Soul
of the
Song

Original Lyrics
BY EDMOND A. BRUNEAU

ISBN: 978-1-936769-13-1
Library of Congress Control Number: 2025902655

Cover Design: Edmond Bruneau
Editor: Donna Lange

Lyricist for:
Robot Raven's Greatest Hits — Part One — 2015
Robot Raven's Greatest Hits — Part Two — 2016
Life Goes On by **Robot Raven** — 2017
Set to Soar by **Robot Raven** — 2018
Robot Raven Rockers — 2019
Kick Back Relax by **Robot Raven** — 2020
Sunflower 69 by **Whistlewit** — 2022
Country Cousins by **The Cow Cats** — 2024

Previous books by Edmond Bruneau
Prescription for Advertising — 1986
Colors of My Within — 2011
New Hues and Past Tales — 2016
The Totem — 2018
Walla Walla Sweet — 2021
Sip & Savor — 2023

*For all the gifted musicians
who have crafted melodies
to make my words
into produced songs.*

Thank you for your talent.

FORWARD

The first lyric I wrote was for a **Buckeroo Bagels** jingle with music and vocals by the great Bruce Innes — who garnered fame with the song, *One Tin Soldier* with his group, **The Original Caste**. Over the years, we worked together on many jingle projects with a variety of clients.

After I produced **Abiqua's** album, *Abiqua Remastered* and **John Rigg's** two solo efforts, *Rigged* and *Folk Fresco* — we got to talking about what to do next. We began writing songs together, the very first being, *World Class Bullies*. In the end, the collaboration yielded four complete albums and four singles. John Rigg is as imaginative and proficient as anyone I've ever encountered in the music industry and every time I listen to a **Robot Raven** song, I am in awe of his enormous talent and versatility.

I began to think about a concept formulating in my mind for a year or two — an homage to the musical revolution and free spirit of the late 1960's and early 1970's. So, I started writing some lyrics to songs I felt fit the era. Once *Supernaturally High*, *Lavender Love-In,* and *H'ashbury (Haight-Asbury)* — among others — were complete, I discovered a fresh musical talent living in Italy named Michele Zara, who agreed to partner with me on the project. With his extensive creative efforts, *Sunflower 69* by **Whistlewit** was born. The last song on the album had a different production by another wonderful musical duo, Jürgen Geppert and Petra Stief from Germany, who found a song in a poem I wrote about Joni Mitchell — *Joni*.

After that experience, I thought I'd delve into the world of country music and see what happens. I was fortunate to touch base with musician extraordinaire Daryl Myers from Mobile, Alabama, who definitely had the chops to make my lyrics come alive. Together, we created *Country Cousins* by **The Cow Cats** with a variety of interesting themes — from the tongue-in-cheek *Thirsty University*, the "dog song" *Jackson* and a tribute to *Downtown Nashville Tennessee*. I even indulged my pickleball obsession with the tune, *A Dinkin' Problem (The Pickleball Song)*.

Soul of the Song is arranged by the latest songs first, the opposite of the way I've explained my musical history. I hope you enjoy all my lyrics and the songs that they became. There's a great story inside each one. Go to to **edmondbruneau.com** and listen to all of them!

Edmond Bruneau

TABLE OF CONTENTS

8 **Country Cousins/The Cow Cats**
9 Thirsty University
10 Let's Get Lost
11 Almost, Almosts
12 Baby, Maybe
13 Lotto Dreams
14 Jackson
15 Where There's a Will,
    There's a Way
16 How Did I Find You?
17 Downtown Nashville Tennessee
18 With a Whistle,
    Whiskey and Why
19 Just My Age
20 A Dinkin' Problem
    (The Pickleball Song)
21 Album Review

22 **Sunflower 69/Whistlewit**
23 Run to the Rainbow
24 Supernaturally High
25 Lavender Love-In
26 Make Love, Not War
27 Someone
28 Our Turn
29 Using You
29 H'ashbury (Haight-Ashbury)
30 Rock It!
32 Opposites Attract
33 It Don't Work that Way
34 Frets and Regrets
35 Joni

36 **Set to Soar/Robot Raven**
37 A Girl Like You
38 Hold Me
39 The Little Things
40 Ready Now
41 Password
42 Me 2
43 This Time Around
44 Children of the Universe
45 100 Mile Mormon
46 While the Gettin's Good
47 Attraction
48 Don't Wait it 'til I'm Dead
49 Album Review

50 **Life Goes On/Robot Raven**
51 Life Goes On
52 When Loving Right is Wrong
53 If I Can't Laugh
54 Turn Me On
55 Next Best Thing
56 Rub Her Soul
57 You Know I Want You
58 Text Me, Don't Sext Me
59 Blessing and a Curse
60 Make Someone Happy
61 Always Had the Power

62 **Greatest Hits — Part Two**
   Robot Raven
63 Screwed Again
64 Leap of Faith
65 The Sky's the Limit
66 Nevermore
67 Party Lines, Party Lies
68 Mr. Inappropriate
69 Ricochet
70 Two Heads, One Heart
71 Winter's on My Mind
72 Second Chance
73 Dreamacres
74 Earworms
75 I Want to Know You
76 Summertime
77 Tonight
78 Crank It Out
79 Together
80 I Still Like You
81 Album Review

82 **Greatest Hits — Part One**
   Robot Raven
83 Meet Me in the Middle
84 Something's Got to Give
85 Who I Gotta Be
86 World Class Bullies
87 Cup Half Full
88 Don't Shine Me On
89 Three Bar Blues
90 DNA
91 Kick Back Relax
92 Hoodrat
93 Why Don't You Call?
94 Goodbye Elvis
95 Half a Mind
96 What Tomorrow Brings
97 Finger Lickin'
98 Living to Dream
99 Don't Kill the Messenger
100 One More Day, Forever
101 Album Review

102 **The Singles**
103 Rule of Law
104 Saving Cinderella
105 Catfish Blues
106 No Regrets
107 Runaway

108 **Sunflower 69**
    Album Review

109 **Life Goes On**
    Album Review

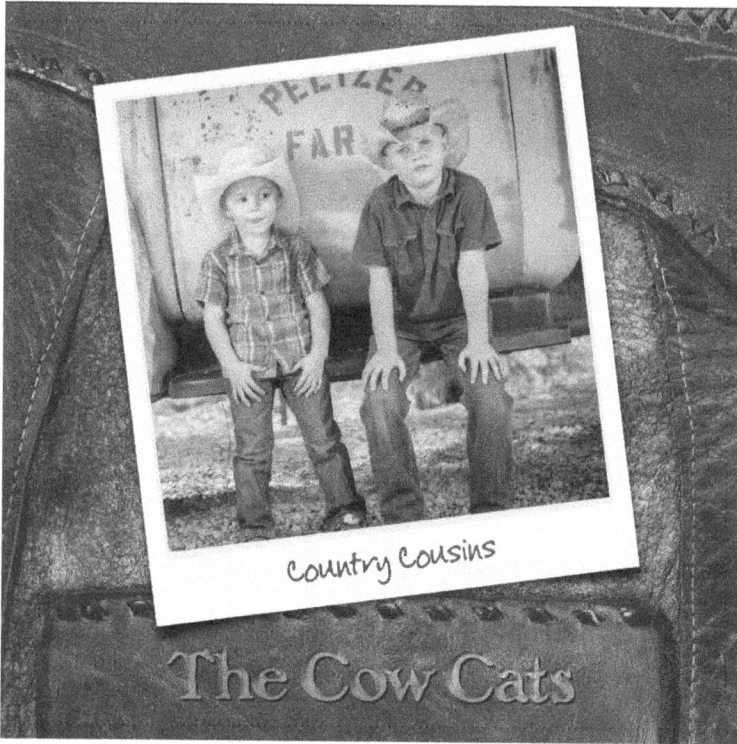

Country Cousins

The Cow Cats

Country Cousins — The Cow Cats

Daryl Myers and I had a blast creating **Country Cousins** with songs that ran the gamut of human emotions. The twelve song album, with its wit, wisdom and honest sentimentality, is portrayed amply by Daryl's great vocals and musical ambidexterity.

It was a fun writing adventure. Although we actually never knew each other as kids, I felt, after doing the album together, we had known each other our entire lives. The album title may be fanciful, but the idea that two people could arbitrarily work together and create such a nice collection of enjoyable country songs is truly amazing.

An album review is located on page 21.

Thirsty University

Friends leavin' hometown — off to parts unknown.
College is a callin' — leaving me all alone.
Folks come up and ask, *"Where you headed, son?"*
I tell 'em *"Thirsty University"* where I'll graduate in fun!

Lager and Pilsner — Brown Ale and some Stout.
Dark ones, light ones — I-P-A's knock you out!
Gotta start in the morning to drink all day.
Stumblin' through my classes, goin' to get an *"A!"*

(Refrain)
Thirsty University. Drinkin' lotsa beer.
Crammin' for a pop quiz with a bottle full of cheer.
Thirsty University. Homework every night.
Get a PhD in alcohol — my future's lookin' bright.

Higher education is where I want to be.
A school that makes everything easy, you see.
Might take years of study, that's alright with me.
Washin' down all that knowledge while getting my degree.

(refrain)

(Mid 8)
Few go to college to be doctors and engineers.
Some have to find themselves before they start their own careers.
Do what you love to do — that works for me.
Sippin' suds with my buds at Thirsty University.

(refrain)

Higher education — always a celebration.
Getting' me an *"A."* Every day's a Saturday
Never skip a class. Don't have to study, just to raise a glass.
Thirsty University. Homework every night.
Get a PhD in alcohol — my future's lookin' bright.

See you in class...

Let's Get Lost

Find a road we've never been.
That's when the fun begins.
Take a drive to nowhere. Let's get lost.
Shortcut not on any map.
Maybe we'll take a new way back.
Afternoon of adventure... Let's get lost.

(Refrain)
Let's get lost. Let's get lost.
Might just find some memories —
Let's get lost. Let's get lost.
As long as you're here with me —
we'll always get back home.

Good ole country bar — horehound candy in a jar.
Pickle right from the barrel. Let's get lost.
Never a blunder — curiosity and wonder
The best companions. Let's get lost.

(refrain)

(Late Mid 8)
Resist the easy GPS. Intuition will do the rest.
Go on and lose control. It's ok to let yourself go.
Where's the risk — where's the romance?
Is there anything left to chance?
We can be smart. We can be prudent.
Or we can get lost.

(refrain)

Almost, Almosts

It's a far way to somehow and no way near to here.
Been so many "just abouts"... it's hard to persevere.
"Keep on tryin," they say. Next time will be the one.
Every day is cloudy — still can't see the sun.

(Refrain)
Almost, almosts. Hardest words to swallow.
Attempts — they always seem so hollow.
Dreams so close, yet so far away.

Almost, almosts — another near miss —
the cards are drawn.
Fateful hand to move beyond.

Almost, almosts — they still persist.
When will they be gone?
It's so hard to carry on.

(refrain)

(Mid 8)
No one said it would be easy. The world don't owe you one.
Every road, a stop sign. Don't mean that you are done.
Rub some dirt on rejection — get back on that buckin' horse.
Race ain't won by abandon, but by ones who stay the course.

(refrain)

Almost, almosts. Those attempts seem so hollow.
Someday, I know they'll be gone.
And all those almost, almosts will be the reasons I carried on.
Yes, those almost, almosts will be the reasons I carried on.

Baby, Maybe

Dating sites all the rage, plenty leaves left on the tree.
How do I know your photo's not from two thousand three?
Pretending you're the person you believe I want to see?
Words n' pics on a tiny screen ain't got no guarantees.

(Refrain)
Baby, maybe, it's the ol' fashioned way.
Get to know our insides out — say what we gotta say.
So much better together than chattin' online.
Baby, maybe, we can see what we can find.
Baby, maybe, I'll be yours and you'll be mine.

Technology is a blessing, but it can also be a curse.
Let's just get together — just dive in headfirst.
Don't need a dating app to tap the magic we might be.
Right from the start — you be you and me be me.

(refrain)

(Mid 8)
I need someone who's real and true.
Are you out there? It's far overdue.
Someone who listens, someone who smiles.
Someone who makes it all worthwhile.
Don't want to swipe — don't want to click.
Do it "old school" — without a script.
We'll figure out the right things to say.
Romance is just a word until it gets underway.

Can't stare at your eyes, familiarize with one another.
Or hear you laugh from a photograph — how can we discover
a common thread to go ahead, together if we blend.
Since time began, hand in hand, let our love ascend.

(refrain)

Baby, maybe. Baby, maybe. Baby, maybe.
Baby, maybe we can see what we can find.
Baby, maybe, I'll be yours and you'll be mine.
Yes, I'll be yours and you'll be mine.

Lotto Dreams

If I won the lottery, tell you what I'd do —
Buy a big fancy car — one for me and you.
If I won the lottery, bills would go away.
Don't need the job no more. Say goodbye tired workdays.

(Refrain 1)
Lightning strikes the lucky, makes it right as rain.
Whole lot of Lotto dreams swirlin' in my brain.
Ain't no dreams at all when you got no way to win.
Snowballs in hell can happen — two bucks, a ticket in.

If I won the lottery, I'd buy the place a round.
First one's on me, *yippie!* Share the luck I found.
Swimmin' pool, fancy yacht, big house, huge TV.
Party 'til the cows come home — have a good time, yes siree!

(refrain 1)

Then relatives come a callin' — each wanting a little piece.
Some I never knew I had. Whole world becomes unleashed!
Tax advisers, accountants. IRS knocking at the door.
I liked the way it used to be. Myself — when I was poor.

(refrain 1)

(Mid 8)
Lotto dreams not what they seem. A perfect paradise.
Suddenly, I'm no longer me if I won that Lotto prize.

I like my boring job — buddies at the bar.
Just being one of the guys, leaving my worries in a jar.
Guess I don't need Lotto dreams after all.
All that wealth would buy me would mess it up, y'all!

(Refrain 2)
Lightning strikes the luckless, takes its terrible toll.
Greedy Lotto dreams — nightmares that unfold.
Careful what you wish for 'cause it maybe could come true.
Snowballs in hell can happen — hope it doesn't happen to you!
Snowballs in hell can happen — hope it doesn't happen to you!

Jackson

Might have been a little flat and possibly off-key.
But when you sang along, it was hound dog harmony.
Weren't a virtuoso or pooch prodigy.
I'd say it was *dog-gone good* and you'd agree with me.

(Refrain)
You were always there when I needed a friend.
Faithful companion — true blue 'til the end.
Jackson, I miss you. Loved you like a son.
There's a special place in heaven for our furry four-legged ones.

I think I caught you smilin' when we took a walk.
Might be my imagination — I'd swear that you could talk.
Your tail be waggin' — knew just what you would say:
Let's get out that old guitar and sing the day away.

(refrain)

(Mid 8)
Warbled like a canary. With bark intact.
Friendly with the felines. Singin' some scat.
Yodeled there at mealtime. Right on track.
Singin' for your supper — *what's wrong with that?*

Jackson was always there when I needed a friend.
Faithful companion — true blue 'til the end.
Yes, I miss you. Loved you like a son.
There's a special place in heaven for our furry four-legged ones.

Jackson, I miss you. See you soon my furry son...

Where There's a Will, There's a Way

Lay our cards on the table. Prevention's better than cure.
From the frying pan to the fire, our love forever endures.
Cookies always crumble. Omelettes break some eggs.
If it ain't broke, don't fix it. Love stands on its own legs.

(Refrain)
Put the cart before the horse. Let the cat out of the bag.
Accidentally on purpose — add some zig to our zag.
Birds of a feather flock together — grow old and gray.
Love's a needle in the haystack.
Where there's a will, there's a way.
Where there's a will, there's a way.

If not one thing, it's another — just water under the bridge.
Take with a grain of salt — or pinch of pepper, just a smidge.
Two is better than one. Roots they can run deep.
Easier said than done. A rose can grow from concrete.
Let the lying dog sleep.

(refrain)

(Mid 8)
Country common sense. Wisdom in those words.
Worked for generations. Phrases we've all heard.
Two wrongs don't make a right. Third time is a charm.
Squeaky wheel gets the grease — philosophy from the farm.

(refrain)

Love's a needle in the haystack —
where there's a will, there's a way.
Yeah, love's a needle in the haystack —
where there's a will, there's a way.

How Did I Find You?

Did you hear my angels cry? Did a light lead you my way?
Fate or simply kismet? Were you mine to find someday?
Luck or simply random? Don't really have a clue.
You are my found treasure. Proof that dreams they come true.

(Refrain)
Mystery or magic — it was you I had to find.
Now you have the all of me — my heart, my soul, my mind.
Heaven sent, the way it went — you couldn't be more kind if you tried.
Now you have the all of me — my heart, my soul, my mind.

When we met, I can't forget — the first time I saw you smile.
Your giggle so contagious. A laugh that drove me wild.
Maybe it's always like that — when people fall in love.
At first blush, the ravish rush — a pair of turtledoves.

(refrain)

(Mid 8)
How did I find you? How did I find you? Or did you really find me?
Let's explore it together — we're perfect to a T.
How did I find you? How did I find you? Or did you really find me?
Souls who found each other. The best yet to be.

(refrain)

Now you have the all of me — my heart, my soul, my mind.
How did I find you? How did I find you?
Or did you really find me?

Downtown Nashville Tennessee

Mosey on down for some real country sound.
High notes on the Honky-tonk Highway.
Southern hospitality, boots on the ground.
Get your country music fix the right way.

Discover the bars down on Broadway.
Shops and attractions in-between.
Music pours out and drinks pour in.
Downtown Nashville has that scene.
Downtown Nashville has that scene.

(Refrain)
Can't take the country out of the city.
Country music lover's place to be.
Famous legends — newest stars.
Downtown Nashville Tennessee.
Downtown Nashville Tennessee.

Can't take the country out of the city
when you go to Nashville, no siree.
Music City's ready to meet and greet.
A country music fan's jamboree.
A country music fan's jamboree.

(refrain)

(Mid 8)
Find your favorite country stars at the Music City Walk of Fame.
Enjoy some famous hot chicken, if you can stand the flames.
Pulled pork, ribs and brisket, slathered in barbeque sauce.
Foot-stompin', hip-shaking dancin' where good times are never lost.

(refrain)

With a Whistle, Whiskey and Why

Broke my heart, little darlin'. You were my sunshine, apple pie.
I'm bleedin' Red River Valley. With a whistle, whiskey and why.
Saw the storm ridin' in. No way to say goodbye.
All I've left is hat and horse and a whistle, whiskey and why.

(Refrain)
A whistle, a whiskey and a why. Enough to make this cowboy cry.
Laredo lonesome, filly on the fly. Saddle-up sadness in ample supply.
Now I soak my sorrows with a whistle, whiskey and why.

Clementine, you were so fine. My heart's been bled dry.
But you can't steal my memories and my whistle, whiskey and why.
You made off with a rustler. Nothing left that I can try.
You were in cahoots, no dispute, with my whistle, whiskey and why.

(refrain)

(Mid 8)
Falling off a horse is easy — you just get up again.
When it comes to love, you gotta sink or swim.
Back in the saddle. Herdin' all the cattle.
Deserted and dejected downwind.

(refrain)

Just My Age

I'm at that stage at my current age —
more days behind me than ahead.
Check the gauge, turn that page —
live a life instead.

(Refrain)
Gotta lotta living left to do. Cross new bridges as they come.
Can't live life In the rear view. Gotta beat old destiny's drum.
Love and laughter, goin' by faster.
Get it in before I'm done. It's just my age.

Pardon me If I sip my tea
and linger at sunsets longer.
It's just my age, I'm more engaged
to savor those moments stronger.

(refrain)

(Mid 8)
It's a wealth of reminisce.
Future days, so precious, as the light turns into dusk.
Time I simply cannot miss before it sifts to stardust.

(refrain)

(Outro)
Just My Age. Yeah, Just My Age...

A Dinkin' Problem (the Pickleball Song)

Got a dinkin' problem. Back in the court again.
Got a dinkin' problem. The net is not my friend.
Got a dinkin' problem. End up gettin' smashed.
Got a dinkin' problem. Goin' by too fast.

(Refrain)
Who's the serve? What's the score? Are you one or two?
Can't stay out of the kitchen or make drop shots true.
First one to eleven wins and then stays in.
If there's pickleball in heaven, that's where I'll find some friends.

Got a dinkin' problem. Really in a pickle.
Got a dinkin' problem. Money's in the middle.
Got a dinkin' problem. Lob the ball a bit.
Got a dinkin' problem. Make the baseline hit.

(refrain)

(Mid-8)
In the gym or great outdoors
fresh start, new game, new scores.
Side in, side out, if you lose, no time to pout.
When the poacher pounces, that's the way the ball bounces.
That's the way the ball bounces.

Got a dinkin' problem. Wish I had the touch.
Got a dinkin' problem. Slammin', not so much.
Got a dinkin' problem. Takes patience, that's for sure.
Got a dinkin' problem. Looking for the cure.

Got a dinkin' problem. Can't get over it.
Got a dinkin' problem. I'd rather do a hit.
Got a dinkin' problem. It's all about the stroke.
Got a dinkin' problem. I'll try and then I choke.

(refrain)

If there's pickleball in heaven, that's where I'll find some friends!

Country Cousins Review — Rebecca Cullen

Lifting the mood of the room with their organic country musicianship and catchy, relatable songwriting, **The Cow Cats** kick off their latest album of originals, with the quirky and memorable song, *Thirsty University*.

Country Cousins is an impressively eclectic arrangement of anthems and heartfelt odes combined. The first song is quirky and suggestive, humorous and reflective all at once, displaying the upbeat groove and musicality of **The Cow Cats** on a likable high.

After this, strong guitar-play takes the reins for *Let's Get Lost*, the groove and vocal maintaining those roots of comfort for the project, before we shift into mellow piano and thoughtful longing, for the unexpectedly emotive *Almost, Almosts* — uncertain reflections proceeded by inspiring optimism and possibility.

Arrangement always matters, and the diversity throughout the album is a welcomed twist of play. *Baby, Maybe,* for example, switches to something of an electronically-kissed country pop and dance vibe, with a certain harmonised smoothness and a mighty chorus resolve; a celebratory anthem of togetherness at its peak, and a personal favorite.

Lotto Dreams follows and brings a twist of Americana grit and a other visit of the unexpected for its horn-section. Relatable as ever, the song dreams big and offers an impassioned, uplifting performance. Naturally, one of the album's most memorable hits ,and followed on quite perfectly by the change to an intimate, heartbroken and grateful *Jackson*. This emotive minimalism is taken further still by the piano-ballad follow-up *Where There's a Will, There's a Way*.

Sentimental and sultry *How Did I Find You?* offers a well placed dose of soulful guitar and raspy, quiet vocals at just the right moment, before the western shuffle and nostalgia kicks in for the wildly upbeat scene-setter *Downtown Nashville Tennessee* — an outright hit of togetherness that begs for audience participation.

After this, the live show implications continue to appeal, for the heartfelt and equally engaging *With a Whistle, Whiskey and Why* — the big-band energy returning, the vocal distantly mixed for another shift in dynamic. Then, the guitars get amped up and the rhyme scheme shortened for the slick country rock song, *Just My Age*, before an unforeseen redirection wraps things up at a defiant peak.

A Dinkin' Problem (The Pickleball Song) is unmistakable, good vibes in strong supply, organic and an absolute earworm, with an essential twist of yesteryear musicianship that really gifts it that cinematic escapism to a simpler time. Fantastic guitar-play proves a lasting highlight, and when all is said and done, **The Cow Cats** deliver a listening experience that's been thoughtfully and enjoyable curated. A timeless project that's both fun and provocative to delve into.

Sunflower 69 – **Whistlewit**

I grew up during the awesome musical revolution of the 1960's and early 1970's with fond memories of all the new, innovative songs hitting the airwaves. Folkies got into rock. Rock sunk its teeth in psychedelica. **Iron Butterfly** began the roots of heavy metal. **The Beatles** kept turning the music world on. The whole Laurel Canyon movement delivered **Joni Mitchell**, **John Mayall**, **Cass Elliot**, **Carole King**, **The Byrds**, **Buffalo Springfield** and **Frank Zappa**. It was an amazing time to be a music lover because you could love the complete diversity and were always looking forward to something new and exciting.

As a lyricist, I loved the messages in the songs — hope, peace, love, harmony, and social comment. I thought, *"Wouldn't it be nice to get some of that feeling back once again?"* So I began writing song lyrics that reflected that era. If there never was a song from that counterculture period from the protest mantra *Make Love, Not War*...there is now!

Run to the Rainbow

There's no pot of gold — if that's what you're looking for.
Different kind of treasure, one worth so much more.
Peace and understanding. World with no war.
Riches for the taking. New world to explore.

(Refrain)
Run to the rainbow. Catch it if you can.
Colors coming toward you — since serenity began.
Run to the rainbow. Reach out and take a hand.
Keep it safe inside you. Brotherhood of man.

We come in many colors — it shouldn't change the plan.
Time to show hate the gate and ban it from the land.
Let's all the share the rainbow. Paint new portraits of ourselves.
We all can be a better me and bid our fears farewell.
Why leave this world as enemies when we can part as friends?

(refrain)

Supernaturally High

I don't know this feeling, never had it before.
I just hit the ceiling, while being on the floor.
Captured by enchantment — always craving more.
Emotionally dependent, it's you I adore.

(Mid 8)
You are my addiction, my dangerous desire.
You are my prescription to get closer to the fire.

(Refrain)
Gotta stay high with you *Hey Hey Hey Doo Doo Doo*
You gotta stay high with me *Hey Hey Hey Hee Hee Hee*
Supernatural, Supernaturally high. *(Better together)*
Supernatural, Supernaturally high.
Supernatural, Supernaturally high. *(Better together)*
Supernatural, Supernaturally high.

Be each other's castles. Live each other's dreams.
Heaven without the hassles — a kingdom for a queen.
We take it to the limit — intense and full extreme.
A high I'll never know again. A love full-on supreme.

(Mid 8)
You are my addiction, my dangerous desire.
You are my prescription to get closer to the fire.

(refrain)

It's all so supernatural. Magic's in the air.
If it's a habit, then I have it. Caught the love disease.
Jonesin' for your body, baby. All it takes to please.

(refrain)

Lavender Love-in

Music in the meadow. Peace is now declared —
Sharing good between us. Compassion everywhere.

(Refrain)
Lavender love-in. Incense in the air.
Lavender love-in. Together in our lair.
Lavender love-in. Blossoms and a prayer.
Put a flower in your hair.

Gentle beings gather. Flock without the fleece.
Does it really matter how we tame the beast?
How we tame the beast?

(refrain)

(Mid 8)
Our intention, so much more when we are hand-in-hand.
Go to where the love is. Peace will find a way.
Walk on this earth gently. We can change today.

Dance to heart's desire. Commune with other souls.
Time to put the love in. Lavender love-in.

Make Love, Not War

Will you share my jasmine tea until our pot runs dry?
Sleep under the shining stars — watch sunrise in the sky.
See the colors all around, without a reason why.
Let's walk hand in hand. Kiss with kind embrace.
Smell blossoms in the fragrant air. Trouble without a trace.
Let's declare it everywhere. Every person. Every place.

(Refrain)
Make love, not war. Make love, not war.
Make love, not war. Make love, not war.
Hate is such a bore. Make love.

Friend instead of foe? Truth instead of lies?
Unity for you and me grows and multiplies.
Emerge from our cocoons. And fly like butterflies.
I'll tell you all my dreams if you will tell me yours.
Why fit in when standing out frees us from the herd?
Dig the music. Do the dance.
Up to us to spread the word. Our romance...

(refrain)

Make love, no war.
(repeat)

Someone

Someone left the light on. Someone shared a smile.
Someone saw the daybreak. Someone reconciled.
Someone kept a secret. Someone found a treasure.
Someone saw the blue skies. Someone found the pleasure.

(Refrain)
I want to be that someone — with sunshine in my soul.
With happy days ahead — who's warm instead of cold.
I want to be that someone.

Someone helped another. Someone made it better.
Someone found a new way. Someone shines with splendor.
Someone lit a candle. Someone paved the way.
Someone forgot their sorrow. Someone had their say.

(refrain)

(Mid 8)
It's a journey to get to heaven. It's a walk to find the joy.
Discover your own essence. Cut out all the noise.
Love is not the question — it's the answer we should give.

Someone showed some kindness. Someone saved a stray.
Someone hugged a stranger. Someone made their day.

(refrain)

I want to be that someone.

Our Turn

You had your chance to do your dance — form the future for us all.
Is it better? Have lives improved? Or have your efforts hit the wall?
We're still at war, just like before. You don't talk about it much.
If our system's still run by you, no wonder we're out-of-touch.

(Refrain)
It's our turn, It's our voice — we'll step up to be heard.
Time to store old ways away — questions to be answered.
It's our turn, It's our voice, time to shape what life becomes.
We create our destiny — to do what must be done.

Such a mess you've left us in — so many issues unresolved.
Can women earn as much as men? Has prejudice evolved?
Do homeless have a place to live? Do Vets now have good care?
Why is health so costly when the sick are in despair?

(refrain)

(Mid 8)
No one else can do it for us. No one else can make it right.
It's up to us to lead the way. Up to us to lead the fight.
We're not idle puppets who let others pull our strings.
Our turn to be first in line — bring what we need to bring.

(refrain)

We create our destiny — to do what must be done —
What must be done — to do what must be done —

Using You

Finally found the one I was looking for.
Magic, the first moment.
Want to be together. Want to make it tight.
Build a future — making love through the night.

(Refrain)
But no matter what you think. He's just using you.
He'll push you to the brink with every wink.
Using you. Using you. Using you.

When we're online — it's like you're really here.
Your smile on my screen comes in so loud and clear.
Got the flowers you sent last night.
Roses for our romance — my dating dynamite.

(refrain)

(Mid 8)
I want to come and see you but you live far away.
I'm in Pennsylvania — and you're in L.A .
The miles between us shouldn't keep us so apart.
No matter the distance, baby you're always in my heart.

No matter what you think. He's just using you
No matter what you think. No matter what you think.
He's just using me...

H'ashbury (Haight-Asbury)

Brothers and sisters — come hear the clarion call.
We all were here before, when love was a waterfall.
Find the family again on the corner of peace and love.
We can get together with flowers and the doves.

(Refrain)
H'ashbury. Haight-Ashbury. Comin' back to you.
H'ashbury. Haight-Ashbury. Dreams can still come true.
H'ashbury. Haight-Ashbury. A loving landlocked ark.
H'ashbury. Haight-Ashbury. H'ashbury's in our heart.

Listen to the music. Dance the way you feel.
Be the spirit flying free. Make it all too real.
Smell the incense. Wear some beads. A flower in your hair.
Find your tribe, it's what you need. A place where love is shared.

(refrain)

(Mid 8)
Been gone so long dear H'ashbury. Forgot our way to here.
The golden city by the bay — different than it appears.
Can we return and reunite the clan back once again?
Kindness and understanding where everyone's your friend?

(refrain)

Rock It!

Rock it like it used to be. *ROCK IT!*
Rock it like Jerry Lee. *ROCK IT!*
Rock it like Bill Haley. *ROCK IT! ROCK IT! ROCK IT!*
Belt it out like Bo Diddley. *ROCK IT!*
Play guitar like Chuck Berry —
Les Paul made history. *ROCK IT! ROCK IT! ROCK IT!*
Elvis sang and swung his hips. *ROCK IT!*
Buddy Holly — what a trip! *ROCK IT!*
Little Richard's Tutti-Fruity rips. *ROCK IT! ROCK IT! ROCK IT!*
Sam the man could really cook. *ROCK IT!*
Ricky Nelson had the looks.

(Refrain)
Three two one, let's have some fun. *ROCK IT!*
Back to where it first was sung. *ROCK IT!*
Now the party's just begun! *ROCK IT! ROCK IT!*

(refrain)

Screamin' Jay put a spell on you. *ROCK IT!*
Carl Perkin's Blue Suede Shoes. *ROCK IT!*
Big Bopper blew his fuse. *ROCK IT! ROCK IT! ROCK IT!*
Duane Eddy's twangy axe. *ROCK IT!*
Last name Domino, first name Fats. *ROCK IT!*
Ray Charles — Hit the Road, Jack. *ROCK IT!*

(refrain)

(Mid 8)
Grab a dance with your little doll.
Love it, love it, love it.
Inspiration for John and Paul.

(refrain)

31

Opposites Attract

Some might think we're a little odd.
Opposite of two peas in a pod.
Less in common, lots we lack.
All good, it's understood 'cause opposites attract.
Magnetic attraction's always there.
Plus and minus, circle and square.
Can't be more different, that's a fact.
All good, it's understood 'cause opposites attract.

(Refrain)
Opposites attract. *(certainly not the same)*
Opposites attract. *(goes against the grain)*
Opposites attract. *(really can't explain)*
Opposites attract. *(our love still remains)*
Opposites attract. *(certainly not the same)*
Opposites attract. *(goes against the grain)*
Opposites attract. *(really can't explain)*

You dig veggies, I like meat.
Quite contrary what we eat.
I add, while you subtract —
All good, it's understood 'cause opposites attract.

(refrain)

(Mid 8)
I love you, not a mirror of me. Together is where we want to be.
I say right, you say left, agree to disagree. Unlikely possibility —
but then, I think that's the key —
a perfect match, like champagne with brie.

(refrain)

It Don't Work that Way

I've watched your battles. Struggle as you try to cope.
Wrestle with your demons. Wrecks havoc with your hope.
There's no easy access. No shortcut for your life.
Sometimes you just can't get there no matter how you fight.

(Refrain)
It don't work that way. It don't work that way.
Best laid plans. Another chance.
It don't work that way.
World turns, it's not concerned.
Cuz, it don't work that way. It don't work that way.

You're going nowhere. Gettin' there plenty fast.
Already wore out your shoes from places you have past.
Walkin' in big circles — you've seen the scenes before.
Discover a new direction. Get out and explore.

(refrain)

(Mid 8)
What if there was really gold at the rainbow's end.
Unicorns, fairy dust and imaginary friends.
All the food we can eat, sweets without decay.
Fantasy is fiction, 'cause it don't work that way.

It don't work that way.
It don't work that way.
It don't work that way.

Frets and Regrets

Eatin' my heart out. Drink 'til I black out.
Carryin' a heavy load.
All my frets and my regrets.
Watchin' my life erode. My life erode.

(Refrain 1)
It ain't easy. It ain't right.
All my frets and damn regrets keepin' me uptight.

(Refrain 2)
The blues never lose. Cry into the night.
The blues never lose. Cry into the night.
All my frets and sad regrets — wrong instead of right.

(refrain 2)

Nerves — fried and fragile. Stomach in a knot.
Nothing soothes the heartbreak. Spirit's set to rot.
All my frets and damn regrets layin' me so low.
Can't escape the sadness. Gnawin' at the grief.
Missed my shot at happiness. Lookin' for relief.
Trouble at the door. all my frets — sad regrets
there's more in store.

(refrain 1)

(refrain 2)

(refrain 2)

Joni

I wish I had known you then. Singing your poetry so confidently —
a woman in control. A woman expressing
her wisdom, composure, certainty.
A woman expressing her skepticism, vulnerability, sensitivity.
Just you and me alone together listening to the LP —
lyrics speaking to my heart.

Perhaps, I should have abandoned school
and driven to Laurel Canyon. Would you have been my friend?
Ten years older and so much wiser. As a girlfriend, I didn't intend.
I'd leave that for David or Graham or fellow Canadian Neil.
But I would have loved to know what made you tick.
Learn what made you feel.

For the Roses is still my favorite. Capturing the devotion
of a precocious eighteen year old, with words that shaped my life.
Listening again, forty seven years later,
it catapults me back instantly to that fresh,
frustrating, formative time that helped craft the whole of me.
That helped craft the whole of me.

I remember you complaining on **Miles of Aisles** about
the audience demanding to hear your old songs.
You said they never would ask Van Gogh to paint another *Starry Night*.
But I can listen without your permission, as many times as I desire.
Experience my own starry night — as my soulful reflection transpires.

I wish I had known you then.

Please Note:
Both *"Thirsty University"* and *"A Dinkin' Problem (The Pickleball Song)"*
that appear on the ***Sunflower 69*** album by **Whistlewit** have the same lyrics
as ***Country Cousins*** by **The Cow Cats** on page 9 and page 20 respectively.

An album review of ***Sunflower 69*** is located on page 108.

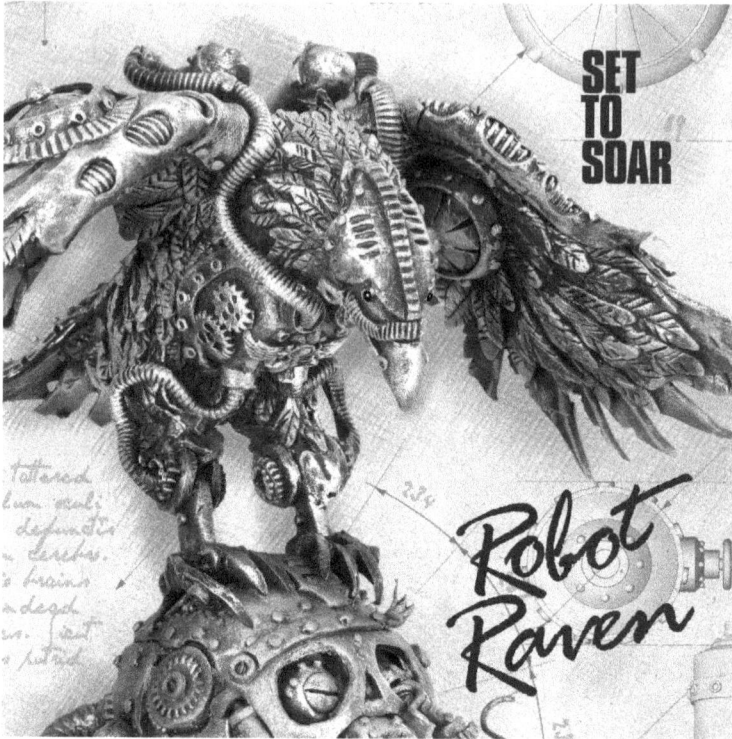

Set to Soar — **Robot Raven**

We didn't know that **Set to Soar** would be **Robot Raven's** last album. It just worked out that way. There could always be a reunion.

We did take the opportunity to explore new topics and musical styles. Song partner, John, sent me a **Ventures-like** demo idea for *A Girl Like You* with only the title repeating over and over. I filled in the blanks and *voila*, a song was born. I wrote *Hold Me* a day after the 2016 presidential election. Other highlights include the tribute to the Me Too movement, the children's choir in *Children of the Universe* and the country-ish *100 Mile Mormon* and *While the Gettin's Good*.

Perhaps it was premonition, but the last song on the album is definitely a fitting goodbye. *Don't Wait 'til I'm Dead* really does say it all from a songwriter's point of view.

A Girl Like You

(Refrain)
What am I gonna do with a girl like you?
You come in here and play it oh so cool.
No matter what I say, I know you'll make me pay.
What am I gonna do with a girl like you?
It's never just okay, but I love you anyway.
What am I gonna do with a girl like you?

Friends say I'm a hopeless case — they wonder why I'm blind.
Maybe I'm the crazy one 'cause I want to make you mine.
Day will come, I'll be the one, that's my whole design.
We'll turn your cool into a shiny jewel if you're so inclined.
I sing these blues so you will choose to make my chestnuts chime.
If you walk right past me, you'll leave my love behind.
Don't leave me behind..

(refrain)

What am I gonna do? What am I gonna do? What can I do?
What am I gonna do?

Hold Me

Thought I'd have to search the world.
Diamond among all the pearls.
A partner who has my back.
Comfort when under attack.

(Refrain)
Please, just hold me tight. Hold me with all your might.
Like there's no tomorrow. Keep me in your arms tonight.
Please, just hold me tight. Say it will be alright.
Close to your heart. Keep me in your arms tonight.

It's you and me, lost in this world.
Swimming upstream in the swirl.
Watching the crazy madness uncurl.
Woman among all the girls.

(refrain)

(Mid 8)
It takes two against the forces we'll fight.
It takes two to change a wrong into right.
It's not easy, but that's why we are here.
Unveil the mask, make the devil disappear.

(refrain)

Hold me. Keep me in your arms tonight.
Hold me. Keep me in your arms tonight.
Hold me. Keep me in your arms tonight.

The Little Things

You may think that I don't see what's goin' on —
the stuff behind the scenes that's goin' wrong —
Waving your magic wand with the little things you do.
Simply can't imagine finding someone new.
Painting with my broad strokes — you're always right on queue.
Knitting it all together, babe, with the little things you do.

(Refrain)
Love is just a fantasy that we can make come true.
I'd be begging amnesty without the little things you do.
The little things you do. The little things you do.

Just an observation. Credit when it's due.
Assembling our puzzle — something you always knew.
Managing the details with the little things you do.
Managing my big fails with the little things you do.

(refrain)

(Mid 8)
You make it all worthwhile. Really makes me smile.
Couldn't do it without you — just wouldn't want to —
you've always had the style — turn inches into miles —
seconds into moments, too — with the little things you do.

You may think I don't see what's goin' on —
the stuff behind the scenes that's goin' wrong —
Waving your magic wand with the little things you do.

With the little things you do. With the little things you do.
With the little things you do.

Ready Now

(beginning chorus) Take a chance on our romance. (repeat)

Time we take our love's next step. Make our moments intersect.
I'm ready now. Ready now. Time we climb the mountain top.
Chime the bells and never stop. We're ready now. Ready now.

(Refrain 1)
Love's such an elusive thing. When it's real it's like a dream —

You want our love to persevere. Want it to last, not disappear.
Just tell me how. Tell me how. You share the feeling in my heart.
Care — so sad when we're apart. Let's make it now. Make it now.

(refrain 1)

Time to face that you do love me. Share the dream and it will be.
You're ready now. Ready now.

(Refrain 2)
Love's a flame that catches fire. Warms the glow, ignites desire.

Time we wake our love's deep sleep. Break the past and just proceed.
I want it now. Want it now. Time we take our love's next step.
Make our moments intersect. I'm ready now. Ready now.

(refrain 1)

Time we take our love's next step. Make our moments intersect.
I'm ready now. Ready now. Time we climb the mountain top.
Chime the bells and never stop. We're ready now. Ready now.

(refrain 2)

You want our love to persevere. Want it to last, not disappear.
Just tell me how. Tell me how. You share the feeling in my heart.
Care — so sad when we're apart. Let's make it now. Make it now.
Time we wake our love's deep sleep. Break the past and just proceed.
I want it now. Want it now. Time we take our love's next step.
Make our moments intersect. I'm ready now. Ready now.

Password

What's it take to touch your love? Is there a secret?
Want to be your confidante. But do you need it?

(Refrain)
I want to know... I need to know... Say yes, not no...

Is there a way to hold your heart? What is the secret?
Can we do this from the start? I'll live and breathe it.

(refrain)

(Mid 8)
Want to know that hidden code.
Your password — your password.
The gate you guard and hide so well.
Your password — password to your soul.

(refrain)

We just talk and use our words. But what's beneath it?
Just at the surface now. Let's go in deep, yeah!

(refrain)

(Mid 8)

What's it take to touch your love? Is there a secret?
Want to be your confidante. But do you need it?
Is there a way to hold your heart? What is the secret?
Can we do this from the start? I'll live and breathe it.
Say yes, not no!

Me 2

First, I thought it was friendly. Just some kidding around.
You put my job on the line — I couldn't decline —
nothing but a shakedown. Shakedown. Shakedown.

(Refrain)
Yes, it happened to me.
Maybe happened to you.
Things aren't fair, I'm quite aware.
Me too. Me too. Me too.

You took what wasn't yours. It's only mine to give.
Should be my choice alone — when and how I live.
Headed for a breakdown.
Breakdown. Breakdown.

(refrain)

(Mid 8)
You said it was my fault. I made you do those things.
Rubbing wounds into the salt, you made up all those games.
A rock and a hard place. Seems like there's no way out.
Can't escape this madness. You with all your clout.

(refrain)

Suffered in my silence. Time for that to end.
Realize I'm not alone — get off your throne —
Throw down the crown. Crown down. Crown down.

(refrain)

(refrain)

(refrain)

(refrain)

(refrain)

This Time Around

I've loved and been lost. Got love and been found.
Want to know where I'm headed, this time around.
I thought I was happy. Been up and been down.
Make sure it all turns out, this time around.

(Refrain)
More than my existence, this time around.
Got to go the distance, this time around.

Maybe I'm too serious. Feet are on the ground.
Don't want it to crumble this time around.

(Mid 8)
Life has just begun —
want to be the one growing old with you.

(mid 8)

Will our love weather when the sun goes down?
Want you and I forever, this time around.

(refrain)

Children of the Universe

Once there was a time we were stardust.
Once there was a time we weren't here.
Spent our time in the heart of the divine.
Waiting for our chance to reappear.

The moment came — a breath of fresh air.
Starting our life with a birth.
A magic place to see, smell and taste.
Passenger on the planet earth.

(Refrain)
We're all children of the universe.
We all started out the same.
Treat this time like the gift that it is —
we all have so much more to gain.

Our garden is simply not as green.
The sky's not clearly as blue.
Let's make it better while we are here.
We have so much more to do.

(Mid 8)
We're just here for a hundred years.
Then return from whence we came.
We can make a difference on this sphere.
End all the suffering and the pain.

Peace should be a familiar friend.
It takes more than just a prayer.
Shouldn't we strive to all get along?
Can't we recall what we once shared?

(refrain)

Once there was a time... *(we were stardust)*
(repeat)

100 Mile Mormon

(Refrain)
He's a hundred mile Mormon, She's a wandering jew.
When they got far enough away, they knew what they could do.
A bottle of Jack Daniels — a room without a view.
This ain't Salt Lake City, hon, no one will have a clue.

Back home, he's a living saint. Virtue through and through.
Passed on all temptation. Good citizen, tried and true.
But when he gets restless — time to get out of town.
Where no one knows him — he can fool around.

(Mid 8)
Back home, she's a librarian, quiet and demure.
Looking for excitement — something not so pure.
Living in a fishbowl has everyone watching you.
Time to make a getaway — a thirst for passion overdue.

(refrain)

Together, a hundred miles away, they shared a single bed.
A secret kept so silent or lives would be in shreds.
Among the saints and sinners you think you know so well,
there's a side you'll never see hidden in their hell...

(refrain)

While the Gettin's Good

Didn't get the hint — never returned your call.
You want to see more of me, but I've put up my walls.
It's me, not you — it may be true, we're headed for a fall.
Not feelin' it like I used to — maybe nothing's there at all.

(Refrain)
While the gettin's good. While the gettin's good.
Won't fret — though I probably should.
While the gettin's good. While the gettin's good.
Don't look back — I wouldn't if I could.
Gotta git while the gettin's good.

You insist on holding on — something that's your dream.
Takes two to make the magic work — already skimmed the cream.
Just one of us is not enough, there's no "I" in team.
Want love to be all fireworks, not the boring old routine.

(refrain)

(Mid 8)
Sometimes we grow apart, no fault of our own.
Change is something to embrace — seed's already sown.
Different person standing here — it's just that I have grown.
So glad for what we had now — the bird has flown...

(refrain)

Attraction

Heard you talking yesterday. Can't get it out of my head.
Drawn to you, feels so true, you're the butter for my bread.
Love your sassy, sultry voice. It's music to my ears.
Say sweet nothings back to me — It's a sound I do endear.

(Refrain)
Attraction. Attraction. Gotta get me some action.
Your plus pleases the minus side of me. Closer to your electricity.
Attraction. Attraction. Gotta get me some action.
Your plus pleases the minus side of me. Love's just simple chemistry.

Saw you walking yesterday. Love the way you move.
Stroll right into this heart of mine with your sexy size eight shoes.
Imagine holding hand in hand, a saunter by the sea.
Your toes touching the soft warm sand — temptation touching me.

(refrain)

(Mid 8)
Must embrace you, gotta taste you. You're the apple of my eye.
Your kiss knocks me off my game. Your touch gives me wings to fly.

Heard you talking yesterday. Can't get it out of my head.
Drawn to you, feels so true, you're the butter for my bread.
Love your sassy, sultry voice. It's music to my ears.
Say sweet nothings back to me — it's a sound I do endear.

(refrain)

Attraction. Atrraction. Atrraction.

Don't Wait 'til I'm Dead

(Refrain)
Don't wait 'til I'm dead.
See the life that I've led.
Don't wait 'til I'm dead.
Hear my music instead.

Robert Johnson played poor juke joints all of his life.
He sang the blues, but never knew his tunes would be so right.

(refrain)

Don't want the fame and fortune long after I'm gone.
Why not make it now and pay me for all of my songs?

(refrain)

Buddy Holly made it big for just two years of his life.
It's all it took to send rock n roll completely out of sight.

(refrain)

Don't want the fame and fortune long after I'm gone.
Why not make it now and pay me for all of my songs?

(refrain)

Set to Soar Review — Tuneloud!

Edmond Bruneau *(lyricist/producer)* and John Rigg *(singer,/instrumentalist)* are the core duo of a musical project situated at the heart of rock n' roll. Bruneau is an ex-advertising executive who writes jingles, poetry and song lyrics. Rigg creates robot machines and reputed to have the world's largest museum of toy and replica robots, located in Northeastern Washington State. Together they form **Robot Raven**. The pair have now released their fourth album, entitled *Set to Soar*. I respond most favorably to the overwhelming technical virtuosity of this group, but I have to admit I really can't nail it down to one single thing; perhaps it's some combination of haunting melodies; the baroque, prog-rock type arrangements; loads of meticulous guitar work; and the rocking nature of the music. The complexity is there, yet, it's stripped back to unfold the melody, harmony and rhythmical nuances of the music.

There are some ripping solos on the electric guitar, and the vocal harmonies are also very sophisticated — a hallmark of the **Robot Raven** sound. The twelve tunes on the album presents a nice mixture of proto-progressive, heartland and traditional rock, as well as smidges of the British Invasion, Glam-rock and Tex-mex.

One click on the surf rock and Tex-Mex crossover, *A Girl Like You*, will give you a quick-paced and diverse listen. Indeed, from here on they experiment and flirt with very different styles, but always in an accessible manner. Starting with the lusciously melodic and fully harmonized mid-tempo track, *Hold Me*. Things get gritty and soulful on *The Little Things*, with its switching tempo and mood. This is a showcase for Rigg's vocal prowess, as well as his guitar skills. The distinctive, delightful and classic finger-snapping rock n' roll groove, is all here in its glory on *Ready Now*. Passionate vocals, the percussive instrumentation and tasty wah-wah guitar work drive *Password* through its paces. Theatrical vocal drama, and the variation between beautiful, quiet, melodic parts and much louder, layered and energetic passages with some incredible dynamics are the focus of *Me 2. This Time Around*, with its acoustic driven foundation and series of melodic and harmonic builds which are nothing short of awe-inspiring. *Children Of The Universe* keeps the momentum going, before sidetracking into the layered vocal delights of *100 Mile Mormon*.

Sounding like a blend between Roy Orbison and Roxy Music, *While The Getting's Good* slides in on a bed of shimmering and twisting reverberated guitar sounds. A tight and carefully constructed piece, *Attraction,* shows many of the **Robot Raven's** most important and typical trademarks, both in sound and composition. *Don't Wait 'Til I'm Dead*, easily lends itself to many an ear with its infectious chorus and bluesy bar-room groove.

It's an album to appreciate. *Set to Soar's* concepts and lyrics are excellent.

Life Goes On — Robot Raven

This is a concept album, focusing on relationships and all the issues and emotions under that giant topical umbrella.

The first song, *Life Goes On*, looks for a resolution in the middle of an argument. *When Loving Right is Wrong* explores the pressures couples have when they don't fit neatly in a societal box. *If I Can't Laugh* looks at depression and loneliness. *Turn Me On – a rocker* in a robotic love affair. *Next Best Thing* is about the desperation of finding someone new. *Rub Her Soul*, besides the quirky Beatle pun, speaks to abandoning control and letting your feelings free, *You Know I Want You* portrays desire, plain and simple. *Text Me, Don't Sext Me* — a plea for honest communication. *Blessing and a Curse* is a hilarious relationship depiction that is often far too true. *Make Someone Happy* explains how love returns when you give it away. *Always Had the Power* preaches about the strength inside to pull away from abuse.

Life Goes On

I awoke and you weren't there...
wondered where you might be without me —
I'm alone, it's plain to see.
Perhaps it's just my point of view,
but argue when we just should disagree?
Seems so strange to me.

(Refrain 1)
Life goes on. Every darkness has its dawn.
Life goes on. Want us to sing our song.

Times you say I don't care.
Really might be unaware, just can't see —
sometimes it's not all me.
Always a perfect pair, even playing solitaire
That's the key — to sailing our stormy seas.

(refrain 1)

(Mid 8)
Lovers can hit some bumps, have their ups and downs.
Why throw it all away when our ship goes aground?
Not broken, but open — new ways for us to be.
Something that'll pass my love. Won't break us now, you'll see...

We're not brittle or broken — our silence must be spoken —
Recovery — will end our misery.
There can be no blame — it's you and I in this game.
Let's proceed. Got everything we need.

(Refrain 2)
Love goes on. Every darkness has its dawn.
Love goes on. Want us to sing our song.

I awoke and you weren't there...
wondered where you might be without me —

When Loving Right is Wrong

I introduce your love in the dark.
I light the fuse — it ignites with a spark.

(Refrain)
Well it's OK, we'll make it anyway.
Gotta be where we belong.
Yeah, it's OK, black and white is gray
when lovin' right is wrong.

I will seduce your fears from the start.
I know the truth when it stays in my heart.

(refrain)

(Mid 8)
What do they know about love?
Unjust to make such fuss.
Can't stop us — can't get enough.
What do they know about love?
What do they know? What do they know?
What do they know? What do they know?

Love always shows that it stays never goes.
Love is a dose that folks need the most.

(refrain)

If I Can't Laugh

There's nothin' really to shout about, nothin' that made my day.
Nothin' I can't do without, yeah nothin' that came my way.
Heartbreak keeps followin' me and I keep wonderin' why...
These times I know if I can't laugh — I will cry.

(Refrain)
If I can't laugh, then I'll cry. If I don't laugh, I will surely die.
Just a step from misery — crack a joke, poke some fun at me...

There's somethin' behind my smilin' face,
There's somethin' inside my laugh.
Somethin' sad I can't erase, somethin' that hides my wrath.
Can't be happy all the time, but I can always try.
These times I know if I don't laugh — I will surely cry.

(refrain)

(Mid 8)
The world keeps turnin' — it's hard to understand.
Hunger keeps on churnin' — innocence needs a hand.
Way too many angels gunned to the ground.
What's it gonna take to turn it all around?

(refrain)

If I can't laugh.
If I can't laugh.
If I can't laugh.
If I can't laugh.

Turn Me On

Turn me on, my circuit breaker — blow my fuse, can't regulate her.
Flip my switch, my neon witch, program me without a glitch.

(Refrain)
My trans sister, can't resist her —
If it's a phase, I'd be amazed.

Transform her into something new. Rivet her hard, tighten the screw.
Induct her to my hall of fame, conduct her pleasure, prevent her pain.

(refrain)

(Mid 8)
Rectify her technology. Amplify without apology.
Integrate her transfer rate. Radar love on our first date.
Tune her in my frequency. Process her with my potency.
If it's a phase I'd be amazed.

Curves are torqued, voltage's hot — my D.C.P. is all I got.
Falling for her magnetic field, her constant magnitude is revealed.

(refrain)

(refrain)

Turn me on, my circuit breaker — blow my fuse, can't regulate her.
Flip my switch, my neon witch, program me without a glitch.

(refrain)

If it's a phase, I'd be amazed. (x9)

Please Note:
This song is also marketed by the name *"My Trans Sister"*
using the same music and lyrics.

Next Best Thing

I need love that won't run away. Persuade my lonely heart to stay.

(Refrain)
Well, I'm looking for the next best thing tonight —
One that won't make me crazy again.
Gotta get me over my plight.
Looking for more than a friend.
More than a friend. More than a friend.

Then she comes and walks my way. Talks the talk and plays the play.

(refrain)

(Mid 8)
I'm searching for a special woman. One who won't let me down.
Stabbed too many times, back on the rebound...rebound...

Don't want tonight to go astray. Need something that makes me stay.

(refrain)

(mid 8)

(refrain)

(Mid 8-2)
Looking for the next best thing. I think it might be tonight.
If I find her, I will know her bark's worse than her bite.

(refrain)

(refrain)

(refrain)

Rub Her Soul

She's something really special. The softness of her skin.
The smile when she greets you. Her happiness within.
This one is a keeper after *"oh so many"* tries.
But you know she must be free when you look into her eyes.

(Refrain)
Rub her soul. Rub her soul.
Best way to touch her is to give up your control.
Rub her soul. Rub her soul.
Never makes you weak, but helps to make you whole.
Rub her soul.
No one will tell you how — it's something that you know.

You want to give her everything her heart could desire.
She doesn't need anything — nothing she requires.
Says she simply wants me just the way I am.
Am I good enough to keep her? Can I be her lovin' man?

(refrain)

(Mid 8)
Caress her with compliments. Flatter her imperfections.
Norish her nurturing nature. Embrace her with affection.
Fondle her forgiveness. Cuddle her compassion.
Massage her mind — try to find her center of satisfaction.

(refrain)

She's free, but comes to me and wants to be my lover.
No strings attached, but will it last? Will I lose her for another?
You want it all, want it always, until the end of time.
Never mind the heart she stole. I'm content to call her mine.

(refrain)

Rub her soul.
it's something that you know. Rub her soul.
it's something that you know. Rub her soul.
it's something that you know. Rub her soul.

You Know I Want You

You know I want you, let's make it come true, today.

If we were fruit, baby, you'd be peaches.
Fresh off the vine, so easy to reach, yeah.
Ripe and juicy — almost taboo.
You know I want you, let's make it come true, today.

Let's make a splash, girl, cause a few waves.
When you're on fire it's hard to behave.
What I'm feelin' — somethin' so new.
You know I want you, let's make it come true, today.

(Refrain)
All I know is love's got a hold of me.
All I know is love's got a hold of me.
Captured me and throw away the key.

Don't you know it would be so complete.
To be together is all I can seek.
My heart is yours, it's all I can do.
You know I want you, let's make it come true, today.

(Mid 8)
Turn around and look this way. Give me just one chance.
You've got to hear what I say, realize it's our romance...

(refrain)

Don't be long girl, can't stay away.
You belong girl, you can't go astray.
It's been one, now it's time for two...
You know I want you, let's make it come true, today.

(mid 8)

You're the one, it's what I've been schemin'
Got to be somethin' — can't be just dreamin'
You will be true — you break all the rules...
You know I want you, let's make it come true, today.

Text Me, Don't Sext Me!

Got your junk mail yesterday, can't say I was impressed.
Want to hear what you gotta say but I'd rather you be dressed.
You might think it's treasure to show your pride and joy,
but it don't give me pleasure to be with a *little* boy.

(Refrain)
Text me, don't sext me. Nothing I need to see.
Text me, don't sext me. Freaks me, wanta flee.
Text me, don't sext me. Jerks flirt to a *"T"*.
Text me, don't sext me. Where's the chivalry?

Can't undo what I just saw. Why did you send me this?
I'm afraid to check my phone. I'm getting really pissed.
Just want to talk, make some plans, dance into the night.
Love is about ALL of me, not just the parts you like.

(refrain)

(Mid 8)
Don't want to see it. Won't really make it so.
Treat me like the one you love, it's your heart I want to show.
Your pics don't impress me none, your play's in the wrong amount.
You think it's gonna get ya some, but it's what you *SAY* that counts.

(refrain)

Think I'm on my high horse? You say that I'm a prude.
Snap the selflies, send them forth and accuse *ME* of being rude?
I don't blow one's own horn, but I gotta tell ya this...
your cock-a doodle do do do will never get my kiss!

(refrain)

Blessing and a Curse

The wicked way she has with me. I don't act responsibly.
Does the good outweigh the bad? Best obscene I ever had.
Can't say stop when she says go.
Shows me things I shouldn't know.
Her evil plan is plain to see. I'm a part of her puppetry.

(Refrain)
She's a blessing and a curse. A bit of heaven here on earth.
A little devil to disperse. It couldn't be much worse.

I like my good in small amounts. My bad only when it counts.
It's a balance then indeed, 'cause both of them is what I need.
So right, yet it's so wrong. Is this the place where I belong?
I'm possessed by her sweet spell. An angel raising a little hell.

(refrain)

(Mid 8)
She's my demon. She's my saint.
Wrap my world around her now,
Our love has no restraint.
Makes me sad. Makes me smile.
In it deep, yeah, there's no way out.

(refrain)

She's a vixen. She's a shrew. Her voodoo will enchant you.
Fool ya with her bag of tricks. All in ways you can't predict.
She's a vamp. She's a flirt. How good does it really hurt?
Always get what you deserve, it's a blessing and a curse.

(refrain)

She's a blessing and a curse. Could it really be much worse?
She's a blessing and a curse. Could it really be much worse?

Make Someone Happy

Make someone happy. Let them know you care today.
Make someone happy. Love returns when you give it away.

(Refrain)
It's so wrong to take so long to say. Two as one, love's easy to convey.
If you're alone I pray, it doesn't have to stay that way, you'll see.

Make yourself happy. Be the one who cares, today.
Make yourself happy. Love — you never have to ever repay.

(refrain)

(Mid 8)
Time alone is not on loan, it's not what love can be.
Happiness is time well spent with another soul, you'll see.

(mid 8)

Make someone happy. Share the love within you today.
Make someone happy. Love comes in wonderful ways...

(refrain)

If you're alone I pray, it doesn't have to stay that way, you'll see.
If you're in love today, you'll never be alone again, you'll see.

Always Had the Power

Set aside who you think you are.
There's much more to it now, by far.
Don't matter who you want to be.
Through other eyes you will see.

(Refrain)
Have I always had the power?
You've always had the power! — it's been there all along.
Have I always had the power?
You've always had the power! It's there to make you strong.
Have I always had the power?
You've always had the power! — to make a right from wrong.
Have I always had the power?
You've always had the power! — inside you all along.

Time to make the light ignite.
Flee the darkness, you'll be alright.
Pull yourself up from puttin' ya down.
Be runnin' when you hit the ground.

(refrain)

(Mid 8)
Don't matter what Daddy told you
or the stuff Mom should have said.
It's time you gained some value,
pull the needle from the thread.
Don't matter you came from 'nothin'
or had a silver spoon instead.
You can change. Rearrange.
What remains is what goes inside your head.

If you're stuck, it's time to leave
no matter what you might believe.
A spark inside will know the truth.
You can escape from your abuse.

(refrain)

Please Note:
The twelfth track on the ***Life Goes On*** album is an acoustic version
of the first album track with the same lyrics as on page 53.
An album review of ***Life Goes On*** is located on page 109.

Robot Raven's Greatest Hits — Part Two

Robot Raven's sophomore effort is a continuation of our initial joke of calling our first album our *'greatest hits'*. It gave us an opportunity to put a greater amount of songs on each album *(eighteen songs on each)* and approach each song with the intention of "hit" quality.

Part Two has even more versatility, beginning with *Screwed Again* — discovers it's only 'friendship mode'. The ballad, *Leap of Faith*, speaks from a god-like point of view. *The Sky's the Limit* would be an excellent jingle for a casino. *Nevermore* borrows a little from Poe with its haunting vibe. Party Lines, Party Lies — a rollicking political voter protest anthem. *Mr. Inappropriate* describes the bad egg in every crowd. And don't shoot for love when it *Ricochets*.

The remaining ten tunes are a delightful irreverent assortment of subjects and song savoir faire — i.e. *Crank It Out* — a lament of the songwriting process and the uproarious punk rocker, *I Still Like You*.

Screwed Again

Broken hearted. Can it be true?
Down the drain, so much pain. I'm singin' me the blues.
When it started, it was shiny new.
Love was claimed — I entertained that you would share my view.

(Refrain)
But I was wrong. Wrong all along. I'm a fool to pretend.
Never should've gone on this long... now I'm screwed again.

Outsmarted. I can't believe it.
Found a place to hang my hat. Now I gotta leave it.
Disregarded, What can you do?
Everything was goin' fine — Nothin' that I knew...

(refrain)

(Mid 8)
It's not okay to cheat and stray. Don't want this show to end.
Throw away my big bouquet — she only wants to be my friend...

(refrain)

I'm a target. I need lovin' too.
A mark who's not too smart — scorin' far too few.
Now we're parted. I'm on the mend.
Shouldn't spend the sorrow, when I'm screwed again.

(refrain)

Leap of Faith

Come a little closer to me. They call it a leap of faith.
There is no guarantee. Not a fall from grace.
Eyes closed, go forward there's no net below.
If you slip, I'll be there, no time to take it slow.

(Refrain)
Take a leap of faith. *(leap of faith)*
Take a leap of faith. *(leap of faith)*
Coulda, shoulda, woulda — have got to be erased.
Take a leap of faith. *(leap of faith)*
Take a leap of faith. *(leap of faith)*
Can't get here without it. Something you must embrace.

Don't be afraid, be brave. Fear won't let you near.
Not the loss, but what you save, makes sunlight reappear.
A leap of faith is never safe. It's a way to change.
A leap of faith — a brand new place that feels so wild and strange.

(refrain)

(Mid 8)
You've got to make the leap yourself — journey to the stars.
You alone and no one else goes through it with your heart.
Time step forward and leave part of you behind.
Pick up what you ordered with your soul and with your mind.

(refrain)
Come a little closer to me. They call it a leap of faith.
There is no guarantee. Not a fall from grace.
A leap of faith is never safe. It's a way to change.
A leap of faith — a brand new place that feels so wild and strange.

Take a leap of faith.

The Sky's the Limit

Life's adventure — a trial at times.
When it hands you lemons and all you've got is limes.
Life's experience — with each one we grow.
No matter good or bad, it's every seed we sow.

(Refrain)
The sky's the limit. I want to win it.
You never know the dice you'll throw.
The sky's the limit. I want to win it.
You never know how far you can go.

Life's a journey — a path truly yours.
No cost to getting lost, your passage is assured.
Life's a gamble — a giant game of chance.
A toss of coin, a lucky hand, a shot at true romance.

(refrain)

Life's a mirror within your reflection.
It matters how you see yourself and go the right direction.
Life's a song — you've got to sing it.
It doesn't have to be in tune, it's your bell, so ring it.

(refrain)

Life's a dream — but not a delusion.
Have your castles in the air, without chaos and confusion.
Life's a privilege — nothing there to squander.
What you do and what you say directs the path you wander.

(refrain)

Nevermore

Raven lives inside of me, wants to fly away.
Flee — it seeks escape. Free — it cannot stay.
Shall I listen to the Raven? I cannot say.
Raven knows you love me, but has it flown away?
Can't put you above me, my heart is gonna pay.
Hear the call of Raven? Fly away.

(Refrain)
A memory I never had opens up the door.
I became your Galahad, you were my Lenore.
Nevermore.

(Refrain 2)
Raven, can you hear me? I know I hear your call.
Why do you keep finding me when you're not here at all?

(refrain)

Raven fights for his own cause. Maybe not my own.
Freedom gained, but what is lost when all is left is bones?
Wish away the Raven? Fly away home.

(refrain 2)

Nevermore.
Nevermore.
Nevermore.
Nevermore.
Nevermore.
Nevermore.

Party Lines, Party Lies

Come and join our party. Get in the party line.
Can't win without you. The one to get behind.
Come and join our party. It's the place to be.
Better than the others. From sea to shining sea.

(Refrain)
Politics as usual. *Party lines. Party lies.*
Everything is crucial. *Party lines. Party lies.*
Won't except refusal. *Party lines. Party lies.*
Want your approval.

Come and join our party. Be it red or blue.
Campaign for the party line. Our version of the truth.
Come and join our party. It's presidential time.
Leader of the free world. Cast your vote in kind.

(Mid 8)
Do we reap from what we sow with choices never clear?
Are you a friend or are you foe? Where do we go from here?
What if we erase the lines that divide us all?
It's time our votes align and put the parties in the dark.

(refrain)

Let's not join the party. Let's not play this game.
The one percent still gets the rent while we go down the drain.
Let's not join the party. Let's decide to disagree.
There's gotta be a better way to choose how to be free.
Gotta be a better way to choose how to be free.
Gotta be a better way to choose how to be free.

Mr. Inappropriate

Genuine embarrassment, doesn't even try.
A jerk at wreckin' everything. A clown in disguise
On a cell in front of you, fighting with his wife.
T-M-I — just say goodbye — don't care about his life.

(Refrain)
Mr. Inappropriate — one in every crowd
He's Mr. Inappropriate — head in the clouds.
Mr. Inappropriate — can you leave us now?

Dirty joke for all to hear, words that aren't so kind.
Little children in the crowd disturb their little minds.
Spills his drink — no regret — leaves his junk behind.
Doesn't clean up anything— a pig is more refined!

(refrain)

(Mid 8)
You appear everywhere, leave us all alone.
You're not welcome anywhere, can't you stay at home?
No one's gonna miss you, it's time to say goodbye.
Wish you would disappear, there's times you make us cry...

Opinions 'bout politics, first one to pick a fight.
Knows how things ought to be — of course he's always right!
Always says life ain't fair, cuts to first in line.
Shoves to get a better spot — stick it where the sun don't shine!

(refrain)

(mid 8)

(refrain)

Ricochet

Just one of those days thinkin' 'bout you.
So many dreams that never came true.
Makes me wonder if I ever had a clue...
Just one time I wish I were a cloud,
float over your way and end the doubt.
Rain on your parade and watch you pout.
You know I'd be there laughing out loud.

Can't say I miss you 'cause maybe I don't.
Can't kiss a prince when he's really a toad.
Maybe all I did was take the wrong road.
Now it's time for me to find a new way.
Chipped out of stone, not molded in clay.
Keep the good, throw out all the decay.
Don't shoot for love when it ricochets.

(Refrain)
Don't shoot for love when it ricochets.
Don't shoot for love when it ricochets.
All the emotions get in the way —
Don't shoot for love when it ricochets.

You might say I've done my time.
Served my days in this jail of mine —
searchin' for something I can't find...
But maybe what I'm lookin' for —
is nothin' that I should explore.
Somethin' that will even the score —
a happy heart restored before.

Thinkin' bout shootin' blanks in my gun.
No reason to run, won't hurt anyone.
No wounds that can't be undone.
May not work, it's hard to say.
Your're out of my head now anyway.
Learned my lesson the old hard way
Don't shoot for love when it ricochets.

(refrain)

Two Heads, One Heart

When I see a girl I like, my life is not the same.
It's all I can think about 'til I know her name.
She's in my mind so I must fan that lovin' flame.
She must be mine, I'm quite inclined to get what I attain.
Hello honey, smile at me, so I can smile at you.
You're a treat that can't be beat, somehow I think you knew.
Just a word, just a laugh, a simple, *"how ya do."*
I know you're the one for me, so please don't say adieu.

(Refrain)
Just get one chance to make that first impression spark.
We may have two heads, but I know we share one heart.

I'm a mess, can't get my rest until I catch a train.
Got to get on the right track and see you smile again.
Don't know where we're going, it's just a little insane.
If you like me, like I like you, let's toast it with champagne.

(refrain)

(refrain)

Everyone has a beginning. Ours is set to start.
When two people fall in love, it's often in a lark.
Turn on the light please, don't keep me in the dark.
I know we're the perfect pair — two heads with just one heart.

(refrain)

When I see a girl I like, my life is not the same.
It's all I can think about 'til I know her name.
She's in my mind so I must fan that lovin' flame.
She must be mine, I'm quite inclined to get what I attain.

(refrain)

Winter's on My Mind

Without you, it's darkness with you I'm in the light.
Whenever we're together, babe, you know it'll be alright.
Gettin' cold outside, but you're still on my mind.
Summer's gone, it seems so long — it must be wintertime.

(Refrain)
Sunshine, you know it'll be just fine —
but sometimes winter's on my mind.

Maybe it's the season. Feelin' so left behind.
Maybe it's the weather, babe, or a couple things combined.
Summer seemed so easy, our love was so sublime.
Hear there's frost a comin' — it must be wintertime.

(refrain)

(Mid 8)
Fall turns to darkness, summer turns to light.
Love turns to you dear, makes me feel so right.
Days gettin shorter, more hours in the night.
Things sort of foggy, cloudin' up my sight.
Without you it's darkness, with you it's light.
Let's stay together, you know it feels so right.
Sometimes the winter gets stuck in my mind.
Sunshine, you know, it'll be just fine.

Days gettin' shorter now, more hours in the night.
Thing got sorta foggy, dear, cloudin' up my sight.
Without you, it's darkness with you I'm in the light.
Let's always be together, babe, I know it'll be alright.

(refrain)

(refrain)

(mid 8)

Second Chance

I am not a perfect person, there ain't no halo here.
I walk the straight and narrow, but curveballs make me veer.

(Refrain)
I don't intend to mess it up it just happens in a glance.
It only takes a second — to need a second chance.

There are times I'm not myself and say things out of line.
There are times when I said yes, when I really should decline.

(refrain)

(refrain)

I will say that I am sorry, I will say I'm wrong.
I can't erase my own mishap and make it right all along.

(refrain)

Might have been a dumb mistake or crazy circumstance.
Let's begin again to make it mend, then rewind the dance.

(refrain)

(refrain)

Dreamacres

The rooster crows, the sun is up, time to face the light.
Fryin' bacon and a couple eggs start the day just right.
Breakfast's done, day's just begun, make it what it's all become.

(Refrain)
Dreamacres is the place to be, it's just right for me.

I wish I could sleep all day, but that's not in the plan.
Go out and cut some hay — part of livin' off the land.
Might not be for everyone, workin' 'til the day is done.

(refrain)

Gotta plow, a horse and cow, a place to hang my hat.
A gal who loves me anyhow, a dog that sings and scats.
Find a stream, take a plunge, get dried off in the summer sun.

(refrain)

There's a bar, that ain't that far and they know me by my name.
Got pickled eggs in the jar, beer that's made from grain.
Drank a few with guys I knew, tellin' lies that might be true.

(refrain)

(break - whistling)

Goin' home, the day is done, 'nother one come and gone.
Chickens'll roost 'til the morning sun, close the gate, shut the barn.
Rest my head, know it's mine, shut my eyes and dream sublime.

(refrain)

It's just right for me. It's just right for me.

Earworms

Got a little tune rattlin' round my head.
Don't know the words, so make 'em up instead.
Just a catchy number goin' through my brain,
over and over repeatin' the refrain.

(Refrain)
Earworms. *(Earworms)* It should be a crime.
Earworms. *(Earworms)* It's how they're designed.
Earworms. *(Earworms)* My brain's in a bind.
Earworms. *(Earworms)* Losing my mind!

3am, wide awake, Crawlin' in my ear.
Mantra of melody, it's all that I can hear.
It takes full control, wires that are crossed.
Gotta get some sleep. Love to shut it off.

(refrain)

(Mid 8)
It worms its way in that special place you hear music in your mind.
Can't shake it off — no escape, thoughts are undermined.

Just a little earworm squirmin' in my head.
Leave me alone so I can go to bed.
Time for some quiet. No more song abuse.
No noisy riot messin' with my snooze.

(refrain)

It's so wrong, got to get it gone, from takin' over my brain.
Your riffs goin' on and on — driving me insane!

(refrain)

I Want to Know You

I want to know you —
the words you speak to me must be true.
I want to show you —
the things you do that matter to you.

What will be — is only what will be reality.
What will be — is only what our dreamland seems to be.

I want to know you —
the words you speak to me must be true.
I want to show you —
the things you do that matter to you.

What will be —
(tonight just seems so far away, really hope you can stay)
is only what will be reality.
What will be —
(all the times within my life, never knew it would be so nice)
is only what our dreamland seems to be.

I want to know you — the love you bring to me must be true.
I want to show you — together as one is better than two.

What will be —
(I dream of us as one, there's nothing that can't be done)
is only what will be reality.
What will be —
(It feels like you're a part of me, something we both can see)
is only what our dreamland seems to be.

I want to know you — my heart is yours to have if you choose.
I want to show you — how we can be a flower that blooms.

What will be — *(I'll be there everywhere, everything we will share)*
is only what will be reality.
What will be — *(You'll be my unity, the part of me that I can't see)*
is only what our dreamland seems to be.

I want to know you — a kiss from your soft lips must be true.
I want to show you — you knew that I'm the one for you.

Summertime

(Refrain 1)
(Having fun in the summertime) I got your back, you got your money.
(Fall in love this summertime) You call her bitch, I call her honey.
(You're the one, don't get left behind) Think I'll walk, the skies are sunny.
(Having fun in the summertime) You ride the bus, I think that's funny.

(Refrain 2)
Fun, it's summertime, summertime. We'll have so much fun —
it's summertime, summertime. The fun's just begun.

Feel so fine, sit back recline. Ain't no time to do no crime.
Barbeque, some tasty honeydew, throwin' back a few cold brews.
Out with shoes to do my flip flops. Singin' tunes to my girl's hip hop.
Dance and shake, just don't stop. Got to keep movin' till I drop!

(refrain 1)

(refrain 2)

Go to the beach, sand in my toes. Warm summer sun rids my woes.
Out in the bay, wind for the sailin', I like land, cause I'm no Magellan.
I like sand that builds me a castle. Kick in my face, that's a big big hassle.
Stay out of jail. No rays in lock up. No time to burn, sun block up.

(refrain 1)

At the park, make your mark. Flip that frown upside down.
I swear what you wear makes me stare. Hear you laugh without a care.
Groove and sun, almost done. Summertime, you just can't run.

(refrain 2)

Summer martini, feeling dreamy, hoping for wishes from a princess genie.
Find a stick, roast me some weenies. Gawk at bitches in string bikinis.
Take top down, air through your hair. Cruise uptown to the fun fun fair.
Marshmallow chocolate, give me s'more, me and my gent got no remorse.

(refrain 1)

Tonight

You are here. Holding me dear.
Closer than near.
I know I love you — just you — tonight.
Time to hold us tight.

Here I am. Holding your hand.
You understand.
You know I love you — just you — tonight.
It's time for us tonight.

(Refrain)
When two souls fall in love
it's a blessing from above.
You're here with me tonight.

Can it be, you and me
finding the key to something more
than the moon and stars tonight?
You are the one for all my life.

(refrain)

(Mid 8)
We are both right here, right now
it's hard to understand —
Maybe it's a miracle, maybe there's a plan
tonight.

You are here. Holding me dear.
Closer than near.
I know I love you — just you — tonight.
Time to hold us tight.

(refrain)

(refrain)

We're here. My dear. Tonight.

Crank It Out

(Crank it out. Crank it out.)

Gotta get a tune down in my head.
Wrote a few notes before it fled.
Gotta good beginning, don't have an end —
not the kinda time that I wanna spend.
When nothin's right, then it must be all wrong.
Just need a song I can sing along.

(Refrain)
(Crank it out.)
Gotta be a Twist n Shout —
(Crank it out.)
Break it, shake it, make it loud!
(Crank it out.)
As long as it pleases the crowd —
(Crank it out.)

Make up a melody, create a chord,
Gotta find the sound that I wanna record.
Put a song together, yeah that's the plan,
a little harmony for the brothers in the band.
Blend the beat then lay down the tracks.
Gotta get it done so I can relax —

(refrain)

(refrain)

Didn't get enough sleep last night.
When the moon went to bed, I was still uptight.
Maybe I'm just tryin' too hard.
Playing solitare, yeah, missing a card.
Where is my muse, man? Must ruminate!
Gotta make music, the call can't wait.

(refrain)

(refrain)

Together

Do you remember me?
I hoped we would always be together.
If you remember me, then maybe we will be together.

(Refrain)
Seems like a long time ago.
A dream we had a long time ago, together.
Though it was a long time ago,
such a long long time ago, together.

We were once so young and free,
always thought there'd be time to be, together.
Time can play tricks you see —
the way all of our memories are measured.

(refrain)

(refrain)

I said what will be will be.
Never thought it would ever be, never.
You said you belonged to me.
It's a scene I could always see, forever.

I Still Like You

I don't like your music, I think it's really crap.
I don't like your friends, so just get off my back.
But I still like you honey, so won't you like me back?

I don't like your car, it's a swell death trap.
I don't like the food you eat, it makes me really fat.
But I still like you honey, so won't you like me back?

I still like the way you dress, less is more to see.
I still like the way you talk, when you talk about me.
I still like the way you smell, reminds me of myself.
I still like you, honey —

(Refrain)
I still like you. I still like you. I still like you. I still like you.

So do you want to go out or what?

(refrain)

Like you, like you, honey, so won't you like me back?

I still like the way you dress, less is more to see.
I still like the way you talk, when you talk about me.
I still like the way you smell, reminds me of myself.
I still like you, honey —

(refrain)

Like you, like you, honey, so won't you like me back?

I don't like your voice, it's really out of whack.
I don't like your attitude, you're a spoiled brat.
But I still like you honey, so won't you like me back?

I don't like your house, it's a 4 wheel shack.
I don't like your company, when all you do is yak.
But I still like you honey, so won't you like me back?

(refrain)

Is this a joke?

Robot Raven's Greatest Hits — Part Two Review — Jamsphere

This album is essentially supposed to be ***Robot Raven's Greatest Hits — Part Two***, but the simple fact is that most music listeners have never heard one of these 18 songs. A tragedy in my opinion, for they are truly missing one of the most musically sincere underground rock duos of our time.

Robot Raven is one of the few bands that can be dubbed *lyrical genius*, and this album brings that out. *Screwed Again* — a wonderful opening song, and it's only the beginning. The album goes on to show other interesting works such as *Leap Of Faith*, *Mr Inappropriate*, *I Want to Know You*, and *Crank It Out*. These guys are simply better than the public wants.

If I were marooned on the proverbial deserted island and could only bring one artist with me, it would be **Robot Raven**. Why? **Robot Raven's** music incorporate bits and pieces of sound that reminds me of just about every rock n' roll band I've loved through decades, starting from the 60s.

What differentiates them from the pack is the superb songwriting, the emotionally honest vocals, and the excellent multi-layered arrangements. In an age when bands are just trying to get their videos into everybody's living room and ride the next wave of mainstream radio, **Robot Raven** is the thinking man's band and this album is a quintessential piece of work.

You've got beauty in songs like *Leap Of Faith*, a rather paradoxical simplistic diversity in *Dreamacres* — a unique and unusual musical setup coupled with contrastingly complex concepts on *Party Lines*, *Party Lies* and *Summertime* with its use of spoken word, human yearning in *I Want to Know You*, wry wit in *Two Heads One Heart*, wistful appreciation in *Together*. Edmond Bruneau's lyrics are characteristically haunting — and musically speaking, the depth of John Rigg's composing and arranging is incredible throughout this album.

What is also worth noting is the little nuances they use to distinguish their music like the harmonies and counter-harmonies. This is a melodic, emotional, and sometimes even gritty in places. However, if you want an example of rock n' roll that does what rock n' roll is supposed to — push the limits, forget about the rules — it's definitely worth picking up.

Robot Raven is an artsy, alternative message-making, storytelling band with a penchant for powerful music and telling it like it is. There is genuine emotion in the singing and the songs range from ironic to whimsical — a little disturbing to just plain catchy. What's even better is that the songs never copy each other or even have similarities; each is unique — a rarity in today's era of predigested pop ballads and dance scores.

Robot Raven's Greatest Hits – Part One

"If these are their greatest hits, how come we've never heard of them?"
Just attribute it the band's bizarre, irreverent sense of humor.

Meet Me in the Middle reminds me of an **Everly Brother's** song
that never was. Bluesy *Something's Got to Give* — disagreement
that never dies. *Who I Gotta Be* — a cry for individualism. *World
Class Bullies* holds the earth's bad guys accountable. *Cup Half Full*
has a **Moody Blues** vibe. *Don't Shine Me On* — straight out rant
about a dishonest ex-friend. *Three Bar Blues* — about smoking
banned in bars. *DNA* — a fearful suspicion of modern technology.
Kick Back Relax — 'nuff said. *Hoodrat* — the fate of the street.
Why Don't You Call? — ghosted and in denial. *Goodbye Elvis* —
what happens when your muddled brain has left the building.
Half a Mind better than no mind at all. Choral rounds featured in
What Tomorrow Brings. Bluegrass humor with *Finger Lickin'*.
Don't Kill the Messenger — self-explanatory metal and *One More
Day Forever* — a simple, childlike song that gets to the core of love.

Meet Me in the Middle

(Refrain)
Meet me in the middle, honey, *(if we are wise)*
meet you halfway. *(save our love today)*
Meet me in the middle, darlin' *(if we are wise)*
Compromise can save the day.

You say — we don't see things the same way.
I say — it's too important to throw away.
You say — I don't feel the same as you.
I say — I don't want to sit and argue with you.

(refrain)

You say — we just can't go on this way.
I say — everything will be okay.
You say — it's only me you want to blame.
I say — I just can't play your silly games today.

(refrain)

You say — you just don't want to change your mind.
I say — there's nothing lost we can't find.
You say — you are right and I must be wrong.
I say — stop the fight before it's gone away.

(refrain)

It only takes two to argue. And one to disagree.
It don't get any better to be so angry with me.
So please —

(refrain)

(refrain)

Something's Got to Give

Something's gotta give, baby, what am I to do?
Something's gotta give, lover, it might as well be you.

How do we move ahead, my dear? How do we get past start?
How can we be the perfect pair, when it's driving us apart?

Something's gotta give, baby, don't want it to be through.
Something's gotta give, honey, it's either me or you.

What happen to our love affair? What happened anyhow?
Gotta fix what's broken, babe. Glue it back somehow.

We seem to dance around it, babe, too many problems we duck.
How can we get past go, girl, when we're already stuck?

Something's gotta give, baby, the bill is coming due.
Something's gotta give, honey, it really should be you.

Don't know where we're going, girl. Is our true love outlived?
If we can't move back or forward, then something's got to give!

Something's gotta give, baby, what am I to do?
Something's gotta give, darling, it might as well be you.

Who I Gotta Be

Wake up to that damn alarm, make my coffee black as hell.
Another day to race the rats — another carousel.

(Refrain)
Oh, I wanna win, I wanna sin —
Wanna scream like a banshee —
Ain't no livin' if there's no forgivin' —
Gotta be who I gotta be.

Countin' hours, one by one. It's my only soul to sell.
I can't wait 'til it's five o'clock when I escape this cell!

(refrain)

Make up time I left behind — trouble, I can't tell.
I'm always in the wrong place, wrong time — no tell motel.

(refrain)

As the day comes to an end. My life in a nutshell.
I gotta get up do it all again, you can hear my yell!

(refrain)

World Class Bullies

Intro — *All we are saying is give love a chance!*

(Refrain 1)
World Class Bullies beatin' up on the free.
World Class Bullies will they ever see?
World Class Bullies beating up you and me.

You butcher the beat of history, you teach the world to hate.
You spread the legs of misery, you thrust till it's just too late.
You slaughter your sons and daughters, you tempt the twist of fate.
You jail your political enemies, your foes you assassinate.

(Refrain 2)
World Class Bullies beatin' up on the free.
World Class Bullies will they ever see?
Love is the answer for your troubled minds.
Put away the hate and leave it all behind.
World Class Bullies beatin' up you and me.
World Class Bullies beatin' down you and me.

Well, a bully is only a coward, a skunk without a spine.
Hide in the shadows of circumstance, your credit's been declined.
You're a plague upon our peace, a vision of the blind.
You malign the faith of honesty, you kill accord with crime.

(refrain 2)

(refrain 2)

The Bullies may win the battle, but they never win the fight.
They show the world a lack of care, and just how much they spite.
No one wants a crisis. You can keep your terrorist ways.
Give the people back there freedom, turning night back into day.

(refrain 2)

Outro — *People of the world, smile on your brother.*
Everybody come together and try to love one another, right now!

Cup Half Full

Every day we get a chance to breathe another breath.
Every day we wipe the slate and cheat a day from death.
Every day we make a choice who we want to be.
It just depends how you look at things and what you really see.

(Refrain)
Got my cup half full — better'n bein' empty.
Got my cup half full — no jealousy or envy.
Got my cup half full of happiness and somewhere in-between.
Got my cup half full and I'm fine with it —
with some sugar and some cream.

No one gets to eat all the icing on the cake.
No one gets to have it all without mistakes to make.
No one has their cup so full their problems disappear.
It just depends on how you make it happen while you're here.

(refrain)

When you love yourself, you can love another, too.
When you love the ways of work, it don't matter what you do.
When you love instead of like there's a larger part to feel.
It just depends on your attitude and how much you want revealed.

(refrain)

Don't Shine Me On

Say what you gotta say — not what you think I hear.
Do what you gotta do — instead of being sincere.
I don't agree with everything — makes nothing very clear.
Just want your honesty — your trust back into gear.

(Refrain)
Don't shine me on. *(Don't shine me on)*
It doesn't make me feel better.
Don't shine me on. *(Don't shine me on)*
You're a liar to the letter.
Don't shine me on. *(Don't shine me on)*
I'm not a gullible fool.
Don't shine me on. What you're doing isn't cool.

Can't trust a word you say — caught too many lies.
You cover up the obvious — the rest, deceive, disguise.
Comes so natural, doesn't it? There's nothing to deny.
You're truly a chameleon — the truth you customize.

(refrain)

Do you ever have remorse? Are your dreams just doubletalk?
How can you live within the haze when your words are full of crock?
Can you be real if you can't feel honesty of thought?
Can you be real if you can't feel honesty of thought?

(refrain)

Don't shine me on. *(Don't shine me on)*
Do you take me for a fool?
Don't shine me on. *(Don't shine me on)*
Don't treat me like a tool.
Don't shine me on. *(Don't shine me on)*
What you're doing isn't cool.

Three Bar Blues

Been drinkin' down at Jimmy's, same ole thing y'know.
Got out a pack of smokes, he said, *"ya can't do dat no mo."*

(Refrain)
I've got the three bar blues, what can I do now?
Got to smoke 'em outside — what da law will allow.

I go to Duffy's Tavern, order myself a beer.
Light one up, Duffy says, *"ya can't do dat in here."*

(refrain)

Make it down to Murphy's, she pours me a drink.
Takin' out a smoke, she says, *"ya can't do dat stink!"*

(refrain)

Take it outside!

(blues break)

It's ten degrees, I'm freezin', I should be dere inside.
Frozen to my fingers, at least I'm with ma tribe.

(refrain)

Smoke 'em if ya got 'em, but forget about the bar.
Don't mean to make mo' trouble with my big ol' cigar.

(refrain)

One more time, let's take it outside!

(blues break)

Brrrrrrrr!

Got to smoke 'em outside, what da law will allow.

DNA

There's a code inside of us. Fingerprints on display.
It contains everything there is of me.
Stay away from my D-N-A!
Stay away — from my D-N-A!

I know it's genetic makeup. An original, not a cliche.
Don't clone a damn copy of me,
Stay away from my D-N-A!
Stay away — from my D-N-A!

(Refrain)
D-N-A. D-N-A.
Don't want no one cloning me —
D-N-A. D-N-A.

Not the genes I want to wear. Forensics can go away.
I'm not an enzyme to formulate.
Stay away from my D-N-A!
Stay away — from my D-N-A!

They know too much already. Must keep the wolves at bay.
They already know my soul online.
Stay away from my D-N-A!
Stay away — from my D-N-A!

(refrain)

I ain't no criminal. No reason I should obey.
It's a crutch, they just can't know so much!
Stay away from my D-N-A!
Stay away — from my D-N-A!

Big science sacrifice — I feel like I'm on display.
One false move and they've got me now —
Stay away from my D-N-A!
Stay away — from my D-N-A!

(refrain)

Kick Back Relax

I think I'll just kick back a while.
Relaxation to help the smile.
The days are long, but not long enough.
Seems there's always too much stuff to do —
Today — just sit back relax.
Tonight — to sleep — just dream to the max.
Tomorrow brings another day.
A chance to sing — to dance — to play.
I think I'll just kick back relax today.

The sun is up. I know somewhere.
Let's walk the path without a care.
The day has come, let's have some fun.
A lovely night for everyone.
I hear some music playing there.
Smells from the past that make me care.
I can't recall, I have some doubt.
I only know it's what it's all about.
I think I'll just kick back relax today.

I think I'll just kick back a while.
Relaxation to help the smile.
The days are long, but not long enough.
Seems there's always too much stuff to do —
Today — just sit back relax.
Tonight — to sleep — just dream to the max.
Tomorrow brings another day.
A chance to sing — to dance — to play.
I think I'll just kick back relax today.

Hoodrat

She's just a girl who likes to hang. A girl who can provide.
The gang don't like no hanger ons. So, she takes 'em for a ride.

(Refrain)
Hoodrat, hoodrat, baby, looking to hang with the gang.
Hoodrat, hoodrat, yeah — now she knows how big is the bang!

Found her friends just down the street. They said they liked her fine.
She's off the track and can't get back. Now her life is on the line.

(refrain)

She once was pretty, oh so fine, gave the teachers a smile.
Now she's lost most everything, livin' the gangsta style.

(refrain)

(refrain)

Some call 'em the brotherhood, the boyz, the bloods, the tribe.
Wait and see just what's in store and how long you'll be alive.

(final refrain)
Hoodrat, hoodrat, baby, hookin' up now with the gang.
Hoodrat, hoodrat, yeah — livin' to die with a bang!
Hoodrat, hoodrat, baby — gangin' up with a bang!
Hoodrat, hoodrat, yeah — now she knows how big is the bang!

Why Don't You Call?

you have no new messages...

(Refrain)
Why don't you call? *(Why don't you call?)*
I'm sittin' here waiting, beating my head against the wall.
Why don't you call? *(Why don't you call?)*
I'm thinking' something's wrong 'cause your silence says it all.
Yeah, why don't you call?

I left a message this mornin' —
thought we had a good thing goin'.
Why don't you call? Why'd we drop the ball?
Why don't you call me again?

(refrain)

Seems uncool to call back again,
Seems waiting turns to torture instead.
Why don't you call? The time just crawls...
Why don't you call me again?

(refrain)

(Mid 8)
Is your phone on the blink?
Is poor reception causing this stink?
Why don't you call? Did you take a fall?
Why don't you call me again?

(refrain)

(refrain)

Left another message this mornin' —
Thought we had a good thing goin'. Why don't you call?
It makes me feel so small — why don't you call me again?

(refrain)

Why don't you call? *(Why don't you call?)*
I'm sittin' here waiting, beating my head against the wall.

Goodbye Elvis

My brain has left the building to a place unknown.
My brain has left the building, so I just sit and moan —
My brain has left the building, can't be reached by phone.

(Refrain)
Say, hey. *(hey)* Lost a day. *(hey)*
Can't remember where I stay.
Or even how I got this way. *(hey)*
Tryin' to think of somethin' to say —
Goodbye Elvis and my heart, maybe that's a start!

My brain has left the building, may have left too soon.
My brain has left the building, I'm stuck in this damn room.
My brain has left the building on the dark side of the moon.

(refrain)

My brain has left the building, no longer on the stage.
My brain has left the building, just won't act its age.
My brain has left the building, words have left the page.

(refrain)

My brain is in the building, I'll keep it in a sack.
My brain is in the building, it's important, that's a fact!
My brain is in the building, so glad to have it back!

(refrain)

Half of Mind

I've got half of mind that tells me where to go.
I've got half of mind that makes me lose control…
A panic attack just takes me back,
there's no place left to go —
It's not what you feel, it's what you know.

I've got half of mind that tells me what to do.
I've got half of mind that makes me come unglued.
Then comes anxiety — a bad trip from my brain.
Oh, don't you know, I'm going insane?

(Refrain)
If half a mind is all I have, half a mind just ain't bad.
Take back my half of mind and get me to the truth...
I've got to get back in the groove.

I've got half of mind that tells me what to feel.
I've got half of mind — don't know what is real.
Just can't seem to get to sleep, I'm afraid to shut my eyes...
I'm full of fear, hear my cries!

I've got half of mind that beats me when I'm down.
I've got half of mind, but can't get off the ground.
Then creeps in the doubt for listening to my brain —
Oh, don't you know, I've gone insane?

(refrain)

I've got half of mind, but I think it's comin' due.
I've got half of mind and I just don't have a clue.
I've got half of mind when I'm there with you.
I've got half of mind — just can't breakthrough…
I've got half of mind, watch out down below!
I've got half of mind that's goin' to blow...

What Tomorrow Brings

I sang a song 'til way past dawn,
'til way past dawn you sang with me...
I wonder what tomorrow brings?

(Refrain)
Time enough today. Time enough to stay.
Time enough to say goodbye...

Well, what's the take on the latest news?
And does it make you sing the blues?
Has it gone a bit too far or will it even leave a scar?
I wonder what tomorrow brings?

If it has come to pass that you are living in the past,
then take some action, don't run fast for life is but a dream...
The money woes when the money goes,
your greed for life it really shows —
Don't look back, just run with the pack and then you fade away...

We sang a song a bit too long, a bit too long you sang with me.
I wonder what tomorrow brings?

(refrain, repeat verse in round fashion)

Well, what's the take on the latest news?
And does it make you sing the blues?
Has it gone a bit too far or will it even leave a scar?
I wonder what tomorrow brings??

(repeat in round fashion with previous verse)

Finger Lickin'

I first saw her down the street, said, *"You're lookin' fine!"*
There's a spot I'd love to meet, a place where we could dine.

(Refrain)
She's a big plate of chicken, a side of beans and rice.
She's enough to whet my appetite,
enough to add some spice.
She's finger-lickin', finger-pickin', finger-frickin' goooooooood!

I asked her what she'd like to drink, said, "I'd like some wine!"
First one got sucked down so fast, put a tingle in my spine!

(refrain)

C'mon you all know the words!

(crowd refrain)

After that I walked her home, said, *"Could I come inside?"*
She just smiled, took my hand, said, *"I thought that was implied!"*

(refrain)

When I woke to sweet sunshine, said, *"Really was devine!"*
She remarked, *"It ain't over yet, let's do it one more time!"*

(refrain)

(refrain)

Living to Dream

Living to dream...

Life doesn't bother what you believe.
Your wealth and fame don't count.
I'm caught inbetween, you see.
I'm living to dream. Living to dream.

There are things that I dream to do that seem quite extreme.
Yes, I'm seeing it sight unseen.
I'm living to dream. Living to dream. Dream. Dream.

I can dream anything that I want and make it all come true.
I'll always be there with you.
I'm living to dream. Living to dream.

Peace comes from within your dreams and love comes from you.
Make the most of what time you have left.
I'm living to dream. Living to dream.

Life doesn't bother what you believe.
Your wealth and fame don't count.
I'm caught inbetween, you see. I'm living to dream.

Don't Kill the Messenger

(Refrain)
Don't kill the messenger, let the heart speak free.
Don't kill the messenger, there's no reason to blame me.

You said you wanted honesty — you said you wanted truth.
Whether it was right or wrong, sometimes it's not so smooth.
Now my phone is never ringing, my texts get no reply.
Don't punish the one who told you about facts you can't deny.

(refrain)

It didn't paint a pretty picture, It wasn't a charming scene —
you might have meant it clever, but it came out really mean.
I thought we trusted one another and had each other's backs.
I said something you can't handle, now I'm paying the terminal tax.

(refrain)

Easy to say the gentle junk — the stuff you want to hear,
but there's times you just gotta know things unpleasant to the ear.
Blame the one who started it, not by what was said.
When you kill the messenger, you're killing me, instead.

(refrain)

(refrain)

(refrain)

One More Day Forever

(Refrain 1)
Just one more day, yes, one more day. One more day forever...

And If I stay, will you stay too? So we can play together.
And If I smile, will you smile too? So we can laugh together.

(refrain 1)

(refrain 1)

If I'm sad, will you cry too? And hold me 'til I'm better?
And If I fall, will you come through? So many storms to weather.

(refrain 1)

(refrain 1)

And If we love and don't look back, our lives will be a treasure.
And If I share my life with you, will you be mine forever?

(refrain 1)

(refrain 1)

And if I sing my song for you, it'll always gives us pleasure.
And if you share your life with me, then I'll be your's forever.

(Refrain 2)
Just one more day, yes, one more day. One more day together...
Just one more day, yes, one more day. One more day forever...

Robot Raven's Greatest Hits — Part One Review — James Sander

Methadone for the Death of Rock and Roll

Like most people of a certain age, I grew up on FM radio. From the time I was able to tune in a rock and roll station I was listening to the standards of the 60's. They were not exactly the songs of my generation, rather those of my older siblings, but nonetheles,s these tunes were firmly cemented into my head as a foundation. *The Beatles, the Stones, Beach Boys, Zeppelin, Clapton.* The ear worms of an epoch. FM stations played them non stop until the unceasing march of time declared them actually *"oldies."*

I went to college and began a questionable affair with new wave and punk, but constantly was drawn to the now gracefully decaying songs that I had first heard in my rec room as a kid, coming from my brother's room. When no one was around, like in my car, I would covertly turn up the radio on classic songs that would have made my mohawked friends cringe. Lets be honest: we have all heard that stuff too many times. It's like a popsicle being preserved at the Smithsonian, easy to love for an afternoon, but it is not necessarily an heirloom.

What was fun about **Robot Raven** to me was that fact that it unabashedly echos the sound and harmonies of many of those songs. While not always reaching the zenith, it does give comfort to those of us missing the novelty of that popsicle's flavor we have tired of from repeated licks.

With ***Robot Raven's Greatest Hits — Part One***, I heard bits of *the Byrds*, some proto-psychadelia, British blues rockers of the 70's and beyond. **Robot Raven** was actually pretty good. Some cuts were really fun. *(Don't Shine Me On, DNA, What Tomorrow Brings.)* It wasn't exactly the real thing, but it was comforting to hear something new that proved the original enjoyment of many years ago wasn't misspent. An injection of calming sedative to make the impending death of the music we once loved more palatable. Pallative Rock? *Greatest Hits* might be an ironic title, but then again they did seem to study such things carefully. Good show lads.

RULE OF LAW
WHISTLEWIT

Saving Cinderella
ROBOT RAVEN

ROBOT RAVEN
Catfish Blues

No Regrets
ROBOT RAVEN

Runaway
Robot Raven

The Singles – Whistlewit & Robot Raven

Sometimes a song just can't wait for an album to be released —
too timely and important. Or it couldn't fit within time or placement
restraints. Nevertheless, every song is important and deserves the
chance to stand on its own two feet.

Rule of Law

Woke up this morning with somethin' in my craw —
seems it's gettin' popular to question our Rule of Law.
Justice is the foundation for our land of the free —
it applies to everyone — no exceptions, no *"not me's"*.

(Refrain)
Rule of Law. Rule of Law.
Right over wrong. Our eagle has claws.
Law of the land sings its serenade.
Mess with the U.S. — penance gets paid.
Rule of Law.

We all have opinions about how things run.
How we vote determines what we want done.
Let's not ignore the constitution at its very core —
throw due process out the window, show liberty the door!

Courts are fair and honest. Backbone of our truth.
Innocent until guilty — that's when they find the proof.
Society's redemption when danger and trouble lurk.
Do the crime. Do the time. That's the way it works.

(refrain)

(Mid 8)
Stand up, America, for things that are right.
Equality. Integrity. Values that unite.
Rule of Law, can't withdraw from justice in the land.
Without Rule of Law — turmoil, chaos and quicksand.

(refrain)

Rule of Law must prevail.
Then the bad guys go to jail.
Rule of Law.

Saving Cinderella

Living out my fairy tale at last.
Learned my lessons from my troubled past.

(Refrain)
I'm saving Cinderella,
she's the one who wants to be free from her history, with me.
Yeah, with me... saving Cinderella with my love.

Searching for the one who fills her shoes.
Looking for the treasure I can't lose.

(refrain)

(Mid 8)
Is it wrong to wish a prince could come your way?
Will I cause her to stay? Everyday?

I remember how the story goes...
What happens when the book is closed?
Is there any guarantee? Together we will be.
Forever after I can see. I can see...

Maybe Cinderella's saving...
Maybe Cinderella's saving...
Maybe Cinderella's saving me.
Ohhh, yeah...
Maybe Cinderella's saving me.

Catfish Blues

Catfish swimmin' in muddy pool.
Fishin' around, now I'm the fool.
Reeled me in being someone you are not.
Catfish got me on the line. Took the bait, yeah, wastin' my time.
Hooked and sinkered and I'm the one who's caught.

(refrain)
My emotion got the best of me —
a little loneliness and all the deceit.
Save me sucker — I've got the catfish blues.
Save me sucker — I've got the catfish blues.

There's a lot of fish in the sea.
Underwater is no place for me.
Thought you loved me, but that wasn't in the plot.
Slippery catfish gets away. Took my money, my naivete.
Stole my affection, you're not what I thought.

(refrain)

Save me sucker — I've got the catfish blues.

No Regrets

Would have done it all again. Misery made me who I am.
Won't look back with discontent. Nothing there I would regret.

Built me strong. Made me bold.
Let me see truths untold.
Nourished my soul. Helped me grow.
Learned the things I need to know.

(Refrain)
Life has to be worth living.
Forgive the past, it's dead and gone.
It's nothing that you're missing.
Tomorrow's time is listening.

Looking back, it's been a trip. Love's always a special gift —
the kissing and the wishing. The getting and the giving.

(refrain)

(Mid 8)
I've lived a lot of life on these trips around the sun.
Can't get the moments back — you know there ain't no refund.
A one way trip to who knows where — or what we will become.
Always tried to have some fun before the day is done.

Today is tomorrow's yesterday.
Don't let the time just slip away.
Time to laugh — time to play.
You won't get out alive, anyway.

(refrain)

Would have done it all again.

Run Away

You're so magical. You're the one I will always adore.
Ain't mathematical. One plus one is plenty to explore.

(Refrain)
Let's just run away. Find a place where we can stay.
We'll sing 'n dance and play. Live 'til we're old and gray.
Try — it will be okay.
I — love you.

We're so compatible. My devotion's been restored once more.
It's astronomical. Beam me up, you know I'll be on board.

(refrain)

(Mid 8)
I want to leave the pain and hate behind.
Leave the world where it's cruel to be kind — all the time.

Let's always be radical. Escape where we can always be restored.
It's not fanatical. Our love's nothing that can be ignored.

(refrain)

Love you. I love you. Love you.

Sunflower 69 by **Whistlewit Review** — Dave Franklin

A cursory glance at the title and the album art, and you would expect to be faced with something folky and sixties-infused, pastoral, pop-ish, and flower-powered. Instead, you get something much more contemporary.

This is a *tribute* to the late sixties, a celebration of its innovations and artistic expression; a more contemporary mix of sounds and a broader spectrum of sonic hues to paint its picture. Tributes to times past don't have to sound like they are a product of that era. People don't write books about Shakespeare in Middle English. You don't have to sound like a sixties band to revel in the glories of those times.

So, **Sunflower 69** is dedicated to the creative high point of that decade, just before things turned dark and the love and light faded, but it is written, for the most part, in the language of modern music. Sure, it hits a few sonic references or stylistic touchstones along the way, but this album is smart enough to avoid the plunder and plagiarism that most artists are happy to indulge in. It perfectly ebbs and flows between sounds and styles, eras and energies, light and shade, modernity and nostalgia.

Kicking off with *Run To The Rainbow*, we are immediately presented with a neat blend of analog and digital sounds, gentle dance grooves, and slashes of rock guitar. And if the music is thoroughly up to the moment, lyrically you realize that it's a song infused with the heady optimism of the hippie ideal. We are in need of such ideas and sentiments more than ever as the political storm clouds gather, as the sound of the guns echoes in the distance, as opinions and ideas become entrenched ever deeper, and as the world fractures and divides — empathy and kindness are needed more than ever. Or, to quote Nick Lowe, *"What's so funny 'bout peace, love, and understanding?"* What indeed?

When we get to *Lavender Love-In*, we see the real hybrid of eras in action. This pastoral folk song, full of oriental cascades and slightly psychedelic hues, certainly harks back to the Summer of Love, and the following *Make Love, Not War* is more drenched in trippy, hazy optimism, deft tones and delicate textures, ambient soundscapes and space.

But if you think that the album errs on the side of the understated and restrained, songs such as *Our Turn*, with its squalling, stomping blues-rock grooves, remind us that the era was about more than hippie sentiment — it was also the point where rock and roll was begetting rock, the age of the likes of Jefferson Airplane and Janis Joplin — and this is a real foot-on-the-monitor, heads down no-nonsense, mindless boogie par excellence.

Santana-esque guitar celebrations on songs like *Using You*, epic chamber pop with *Opposites Attract*, smooth country-blues courtesy of *Dinkin' Problem*, and the album's last track with gorgeous folk sentiments of *Joni*, very much in the style of the titular artist. Lyrically, there is an appreciation of the meanings and messages of the music scene of that period.

The more you play **Sunflower 69**, the more you get it and the more rewarding the experience. *Trust me, I'm a music journalist!*

Life Goes On — **Robot Raven** — Independent Music News 24

Most bands morph into a shinier and sexier version of their more raw original incarnation, not **Robot Raven**. Remember, they've already made their *greatest hits* records, so they're moving backwards to complete the catalog. Sheer genius! As they morph into a rawer more visceral incarnation of their shinier, sexier selves on ***Life Goes On***.

Twelve tracks — which they lament, rant and rave about relationships and its attached emotions. Stretching out their legs and exploiting their resources to full effect.

Robot Raven's ass-stomping classic rock template is complete with rowdy slickness — reveling in styles from soft psych and broiling hard rock while expanding to greater heights through multi-tracking and ghostly ooh-ooh vocals.

The opener, *Life Goes On*, is so total in its mystifying choral sweep that you almost miss the song's personal implications about two people trying to get along and deciding whether or not to stay together. *When Loving Right is Wrong* starts cosmic and grows until **Robot Raven** tries to one up anyone in today's field of gusting psych rock.

Guitars and drums coexist beautifully in this band, and some of these songs don't require much else, even as additional elements pop up all the time. *If I Can't Laugh* is splashed with acoustic sweat, toting a well-defined electric guitar riff and ascending with a high-stepping swatch of choruses.

The crouching *Next Best Thing* is at first driven by the rumbling bass, then carved by the spidery acoustic strumming. *Rub Her Soul*, the oddball jazz/blues-induced number, is both goofy and irresistible.

The catchier their songs are, the more fun it sounds like they're having, and who can argue with that? *You Know I Want You* is the sound of **Robot Raven** eagerly and grandiosely taking things into their own hands. *Text Me, Don't Sext Me!* has a female vocal and a wah-wah guitar wrapped into a showtime soundscape.

If you adore the Everly Brothers styled melodies and harmonies, or maybe even pieces by the Traveling Wilburys, you'll certainly revel in the album's closing songs, *Make Someone Happy*, *Always Had The Power* and *Life Goes On (reprise)*, which are a little less rock and a lot more roll.

The songs on ***Life Goes On*** are more heartfelt and seem to have a deeper personal meaning than past material they put out. This shows a clear progression in their craft and an even more intimate chemistry as songwriting partners.

Edmond Bruneau
can be reached at
ed@edmondbruneau.com
(509) 326-3604 (US)

www.ingramcontent.com/pod-product-compliance
Lightning Source LLC
Chambersburg PA
CBHW041930090426
42744CB00016B/1996